PRAISE FOR

THE WRITE WAY INTO COLLEGE

"Jody Cohan-French is a guide of extraordinary knowledge, compassion, and creativity. She provides students with individualized pathways to college attainment by focusing on the personal statement. Her talent and insight are assets that will significantly improve the chances of any student. With Jody's help, higher education dreams can come true."

—ALLISON DEEGAN, EdD, ASSOCIATE DIRECTOR
& EDUCATION TEAM LEADER, WRITEGIRL

"Every student preparing to enter their senior year of high school should read *The Write Way into College*. As a high school administrator with more than 35 years of experience working with high-achieving students, more than 85 percent of whom are planning to attend a 4-year college or university, I know firsthand the energy and effort students and parents invest in getting into the right college. This book is written just for them."

—GARRY W. THORNTON, MA, OWNER,
GARRY W. THORNTON CONSULTING

"Jody Cohan-French's take on essay writing does what she advises students to do in their essays; she doesn't just tell, she shows, doing so with both a clarity and depth not provided by most "how-to" essay books. Real student examples demonstrate subtle differences in writing, and points are made in a genuine and easy-to-understand voice just like she encourages her readers to do. *The Write Way into College* is easy to read in its entirety, yet is also organized into practical and logical chunks that can be referred to as needed, making it the perfect tool for busy students and the professionals who support them."

—LORRAINE HEITEL, PRINCIPAL, HEITEL EDUCATIONAL COUNSELING

"*The Write Way into College* is a must-read for any student who doesn't know where to begin the process of writing a college essay, or, actually, any essay. Many real examples of effective essays are included, which break down the writing process from brainstorming to final edit. This book is an excellent resource that gives practical tips and suggestions in an easy and fun-to-read format; I recommend it for any student looking to create a winning essay."

—LAURA REIDT, MEd, EDUCATOR AND SCHOOL PSYCHOLOGIST

"Jody is a persistent yet gentle master at helping every student she works with find their unique story and individual voice, from which a distinctive and memorable essay or short answer is composed. For the student who is unable to work privately with Jody, this book serves as an excellent resource for incorporating Jody's spot on and effective college application essay writing advice."

—BETH A. LEWIS, COORDINATOR, RONALD E. McNAIR POSTBACCALAUREATE ACHIEVEMENT PROGRAM

"Jody's skilled and compassionate guidance has been absolutely invaluable for students looking to craft college application essays that shine. It's wonderful to see her expertise on the subject gathered into one fantastic resource. How fortunate for college-bound seniors that this book is now available!"

—LESLIE AWENDER, MFA, EDUCATION TEAM LEADER & MANAGER, BOLD FUTURES, WRITEGIRL

"*The Write Way into College* is a worthwhile addition to available college readiness resources. Cohan-French offers user-friendly guidance and practical advice that will assist students in tailoring their personal message while simultaneously teaching skills that can be carried over into college."

—EB GATHRID, MENTOR/COACH

JODY COHAN-FRENCH

THE *Write* WAY INTO COLLEGE

RISING ABOVE GPAs *and* TEST SCORES
with **MEMORABLE APPLICATION ESSAYS**

RIVER GROVE
BOOKS

Published by River Grove Books
Austin, TX
www.rivergrovebooks.com

Distributed by River Grove Books

Design and composition by Greenleaf Book Group
Cover design by Greenleaf Book Group
Cover images: Jane Kelly, 2018. Used under license from Shutterstock.com

Publisher's Cataloging-in-Publication data is available.

Print ISBN: 978-1-63299-183-6

eBook ISBN: 978-1-63299-185-0

First Edition

TABLE OF CONTENTS

INTRODUCTION

More than 280,000 high school seniors applied to the eight Ivy League colleges for admission in Fall 2017.* The average acceptance rate was about 8 percent. Three thousand miles to the west, where eight of the ten colleges that receive the most applications reside, the University of California, Los Angeles alone was flooded with more than 113,000 applications for 2018 freshman admission.**

In answer to the "can you tell me why I was denied?" question on UCLA's website, the school states that every application receives a minimum of two reviews. These

---

* *Ivy Coach*, "2021 Ivy League Admissions Statistics," *ivycoach.com, Apr. 4, 2018, http://www.ivycoach.com/2021-ivy-league-admissions-statistics/*

** *Ricardo, Vasquez,* "UCLA breaks application record, sees steep surge in California applicants," *UCLA Newsroom, Dec. 14, 2017, http://newsroom.ucla.edu/ releases/ucla-breaks-applications-record-sees-steep-surge-in-california-applicants*

reviews balance academic and extracurricular information, combined with information learned from the personal insight questions. The primary reason for turning away so many "UC-eligible" students? Competition. You may be a straight-A student, star athlete, student body officer, debate champion, medal-winning academic decathlete, concert musician, young entrepreneur, or volunteer extraordinaire, but remember: Hundreds or thousands of others, just like you, are applying to the same schools.

> What makes you so special?

Grades and SAT and ACT scores are simply numbers. If you're above the lower threshold for a school, the personal essays are where you have your chance to become more than a statistic, to convey to admissions *who you are* in 250 to 650 words. At some schools, you might have the opportunity for an interview, but the essays come first.

The best—and easiest—way to display your essence through writing is to tap into your passions and what excites you. Fashion photographer Lindsay Adler said that when she finds what her subjects are truly passionate about, she can calm their nerves, and their confidence and personality can then "shine through their eyes." When it comes to your college application essays, your personality, character, values, and aspirations need to shine through your words.

> But I'm not a good writer!

I've heard this line from many of my students. Then, we take a look at the prompts, and I start asking them questions related to the prompts. Some of them reply with the typical terse teenager response or "I don't know," but I keep probing until those blank stares are replaced with smiles and the stories start flowing.

When this happens to you, *that's* what you write about.

In his 2006 TED Talk, "Why We Do What We Do," motivational speaker Tony Robbins said, "When emotion comes into it, the wiring changes . . . If you get the right emotion, and get playful enough and creative enough, you turn people on, you get their attention."

> Bring emotion into your writing, and
> your writing will change too!

The fusion of personality, excitement, and emotion emanating from written words is called "voice"—that *je ne sais quoi* that makes your essays unique. When you write with voice, not only will your readers be moved but they will also remember you.

This book will help you find that essay-writing groove and then provide tips on how to polish your writing.

> Rule No. 1: Be genuine.

Force it; half-ass it; exaggerate, embellish, or lie; and your lack of truth and authenticity will be revealed.

Mindful readers can always sense a fraud, so let your writing be a positive reflection of you.

GETTING ORGANIZED

Times have changed since I was a senior in high school and applied to only two colleges. In today's highly competitive admissions market, most students hedge their bets with at least ten schools. That's a lot of essay writing and deadlines to track. The number one mistake I see many students make in the college application process is underestimating the amount of time it will take. Your schedules are so jam-packed that these applications become yet another item that you set aside until the deadline is looming.

--- **WARNING** ---

Do not treat college application essays like English papers you'd throw together the night before they are due!

Truth is, you've likely only written a first draft of those hurried high school papers. Your teacher may give valuable comments, but there is rarely time in the schedule to address feedback with a rewrite. You take your grade and move on to the next assignment.

Your college application essays, however, must be a *finished* product.

Even professional writers go through their drafts multiple times—and so do a barrage of editors, from line editors to copyeditors to proofreaders. In this day and age of short attention spans, keep in mind that *good* writing takes time. My students make anywhere from five to seventeen passes on each essay. Because they're fine-tuning, some drafts may take only a few minutes. My point: The longer you wait to start writing your application essays, the more stress you'll feel. Plan ahead. Start in the summer, when you don't have school distractions and deadline stress. If necessary, drop one activity to make room for working on your college applications.

THE GRID

Create a spreadsheet so you can track progress and deadlines. I recommend the following column headers:

SCHOOL	EARLY DEADLINE	REGULAR DEADLINE	ESSAY PROMPTS	TOPIC	STATUS	NOTES

Customize this grid. For example, you might want to add personal deadlines ahead of the actual ones.

In the ESSAY PROMPTS column, insert the entire prompt(s) for each school.

In the TOPIC column, summarize the subject matter of each essay. You don't need anything lengthy here, just some shorthand that triggers your memory (e.g., "summer in Florence," "robot presentation," or "gazebo").

When evaluating a private school package, don't forget to include your Common Application essay.*

Some majors and programs (typically art, architecture, design, music, theater, and film) have additional application requirements that might include more essays, submission of a portfolio of work, or an audition. Be sure to include these items in your grid.

Having an overview of the prompts and topics serves two purposes.

> You avoid repeating content for a school
> that requires multiple essays.

In each application, you'll want to paint the broadest possible picture of yourself. The University of California application, for example, requires four written essays. If

---

* *The Common App enables you to streamline the application process at more than seven hundred member colleges; these schools require you to submit an essay based on one of the several Common App prompts (www.commonapp.org).*

you write about your tae kwon do practice in one essay, you don't want to write about it in another *unless* you don't have anything else to say *or* the story or angle is completely different. Those four essays should touch on four different aspects of your life and personality.

The same concept goes for tone. If one essay is humorous, be sure to present your more serious side in another. The entire essay package needs to work as a whole; it should be like a sampler box of chocolates, not one vanilla cream after another.

> The grid serves as a content database.

Different schools might have similar or identical prompts. Seeing your essay topics at a glance points you to content, so you can borrow without reinventing the wheel. Similar prompts, however, doesn't mean you can just cut and paste one essay into another. Some rewriting almost always needs to be done (we'll discuss this later).

Using the grid in conjunction with your calendar is also great preparation for college, where you will be juggling classes, exams, assignments, and activities all on your own!

> Feeling overwhelmed?

Just take it one essay at a time. Piece by piece, your application essays will all come together. Set aside an hour each day. If you aren't disciplined, set a writing date with a friend. You don't even need to be in the same room. Call or text each other at a set time and start writing. Check in on each other's progress an hour later.

You might be the type who needs to get out of your regular space in order to concentrate, not to mention avoid distractions such as your PlayStation or the frig. If so, pack up that laptop or pad of paper and head to the library, coffee house, or park. Even if you aren't interacting with other people, their energy can help you settle down and focus.

As you start to ponder the prompts, be prepared to capture ideas—whether writing in a notebook or recording on your smartphone—as they come to mind. By dividing an intimidating writing project into little pieces, you will, over time, fill blank pages with black stuff.

2

THE PROMPTS

As Maria von Trapp would say, "Let's start at the very beginning." When it comes to writing application essays, a very good place to start is with the prompts. During my career, I've read several essays that were solid pieces of writing, but the students did not address the prompt! Submit an essay that neglects to completely address the prompt or goes off topic, and the admissions folks will learn something about you, all right. Unfortunately, it's that you have poor reading comprehension and pay little attention to detail. Into the circular file your application goes!

To avoid this tactical error, be clear on what a prompt is asking, and be sure to address each point.

If you don't understand a prompt, don't guess.

Ask your school counselor or English teacher, call the admissions office, or do some online research.

BREAKING DOWN THE PROMPT

Print the prompt and read it out loud. Read it again, highlighting key words:

PROMPT

Describe a problem you've solved or a problem you'd like to solve. It can be an intellectual challenge, a research query, an ethical dilemma—anything of personal importance, no matter the scale. Explain its significance and what steps you took or could be taken to identify a solution.*

Now, put those key words into a list. By rewriting the prompt, you will clearly see the points to address in your essay. Note that this particular prompt calls for you to make a choice: Will you write about a problem you *have* solved or one you *would like* to solve?

For this illustration, we'll go with a problem you'd like to solve.

1 Describe the problem.

2 How is this problem of personal importance to you?

---

* This and all prompts in the book are or were real prompts from American colleges.

3 Explain the problem's significance to you.

4 What steps you would take to identify a solution?

There is *one* problem to identify and *three* items that must be addressed in this prompt

If any part of a prompt seems vague, look up the key words—even if you have a general grasp of their meaning. Take, for instance, the following:

PROMPT

Stanford students possess an intellectual vitality.
Reflect on an idea or experience that has been
important to your intellectual development.

I have students look up the words "intellectual" and "vitality" so they are clear on the nuances of their meaning.

BRAINSTORMING

Most students start writing prematurely. This forces their essays structurally and lessens chances of discovery through the creative process. Take the pressure off writing and free yourself by brainstorming first. See what you find.

Let's return to the example "problem" prompt. Brainstorm about those four points. You don't have to follow list order, but in this case, identifying the problem first makes sense. Jot down a few problems of personal importance that you would like to solve. Unless you clearly have a topic, there's no need to narrow yourself right away.

> Size does not matter!

You don't have to write about solving global warming or ending the war on terrorism. You can write about something as "small" as trying to mend a rift between two friends. I'll discuss "size" more later, but for now, just identify a problem you'd like to solve. If you pick subject matter from your own experiences, your personal connection to the material will make the writing come easier.

Now, pretend you are an Olympic swimmer coiled on the block. The starter gun goes off, and you fly into the water and swim your brains out. In this case, you'll write your brains out. For at least ten minutes.

Don't worry about organizing thoughts or connecting sentences or utilizing good grammar. Don't judge; don't hold back. Just keep that pen or those keys moving. You are simply downloading thoughts. Later, you'll cull through these thoughts to craft an essay. But for now—even if those initial sentences seem worthless or stupid—keep going. This process often reveals good content . . . if you let yourself go.

Repeat this downloading with each point of the prompt. If thoughts don't come easily, you may not have picked a problem that is truly significant to you. (We'll come back to what to do with your brainstorming notes in Chapter 4 on "Crafting.")

THE POWER OF A "SMALL" STORY

PROMPT

Describe a place or environment where you are perfectly content. What do you do or experience there, and why is it meaningful to you?

After we read this prompt together, I asked students to write down places where they felt content. I then asked them to describe their place. I noticed one student wasn't writing. She said she was hesitant because her place wasn't all that significant. When I asked her where she felt content, she shook her head, a little embarrassed. I pointed out that she had written down her happy place immediately, so it had to be meaningful to her. She finally revealed it was the gazebo at her neighborhood park; she liked to stop there on her way home from school. I asked her to brainstorm about the gazebo: how it looks, what happens there, what she does, and how she feels there. When I looked back a few minutes later, she was engrossed, her pen moving effortlessly.

The brainstorming exercise helped this student discover some terrific material. She was also able to adapt this material to a similar prompt for another school:

Describe the world you come from: for example, your family, clubs, school, community, city, or town. How has that world shaped your dreams and aspirations? [250 words]

After brainstorming about her dreams and aspirations, this student realized she could perfectly link her thoughts. The resulting "simple" story about a gazebo in a park earned the student early admission to the Massachusetts Institute of Technology:

> My eyes drift away from "Exploring Gymnosperm Diversity" in my biology textbook as two women in hijabs wander into my gazebo and say hello. A few minutes later, an elderly Asian man stops to take in the view of the lake. Then, two teenagers burst in. I'm drawn to the one on the skateboard because I skate, too. They're blasting awful hip-hop, but I like the beat.
>
> I love going to the park after school to do my homework. I prefer the solitude I feel when I'm alone in the company of strangers to the loneliness I often feel at home as an only child. Unlike the chambered nautilus, I like to find space outside my shell where I can open up to the world. As all these characters come through my gazebo, I feel oddly comfortable with them. I feel a connection.

I've realized that these chance meetings face-to-face in the park are no different than the Canterbury of tales I read about online in the "Lives" column of *The New York Times* or while interacting through hashtags on Twitter and blogs on Tumblr. Such online encounters are natural for me, and as a computer scientist, I want to create more of the technology that makes them feel so natural. Through advancements in artificial intelligence, human-computer interfaces, and mobile computing, I want to hear and help share other people's stories, whether on the other side of the gazebo or the other side of cyberspace.

Look at all the things this essay reveals about this student! We learn much more than the fact that she likes to study in the gazebo after school and wants to become a computer scientist. This essay is *loaded* with information about the writer, and it is all conveyed through good storytelling. I want to note that connecting her ideas was not planned; it was discovered. If you let yourself brainstorm and explore without judgment, magic can happen to you, too.

Another student I worked with wrote about the couch in her living room. That's right, the couch. And she gained early admission to the University of Pennsylvania. Now, the couch wasn't her literal world, but the stories about how her family acquired that couch and the life experiences that occurred on and around that couch were. Here is her essay:

The leg is still crooked from the day we found it lying on the street, unwanted. We took it home. I had never seen my parents so excited. When they came to America, all they brought with them were two suitcases. My father was looking for a job and my mother took care of my brother and me, so they counted every penny. Finding something we needed was a gift.

Thirteen years later, that couch is still in our living room. The orange stain on the cushion reminds me of the day my brother taught me how to throw a basketball. He showed me his special flick of the wrist, which I imitated, forgetting the Orangina in my hand, which went flying. My brother and I have spent a lot of time sitting on that couch. We talk about everything: what kind of friends I should make, which classes to take, and what kind of person I should be.

The condition of the left arm has worsened lately. Sometimes when I'm too tired to stand while practicing viola, I lean on it for support. While working on Brahms' Sonata No. 2, I swayed so much to the romantic music that I gradually wore off the paint. I used to play viola like a robot; it was all about winning competitions. But when I played the sonata at the senior center, everything changed. To see the gratitude on the faces in the audience and hear their applause—even though I made mistakes—made me realize that performing music isn't about how well I play; it's about playing with my heart.

The seat on the far left is still empty . . . waiting . . . for my father. After moving from job to job, he finally found stable employment in China. Even though we now live in a spacious house and can afford new furniture, our beloved couch is still with us. I miss my father and cherish when he returns home every three months to sit with the entire family that awaits him on the couch.

I've spent so much time on this piece of furniture it feels like my own little world. Whenever I sit on it, I am reminded of the memories it holds. I also think about my future. I want to work hard like my parents as I start my new, independent life. I want to be a role model to my loved ones like my brother has been to me. I want to play the viola, or do anything in life, not just for me but also for others. I want to be the parent that my father never could be and stay close to my family.

As I head off to college, my world will expand through the classes I attend and the people I meet. I will continue to learn from new experiences even if, like the couch, they have imperfections, because these imperfections are what shape who I am and who I want to be.

So just write away and see what comes up. You are on an exposition expedition!

CHOOSING AN APPROPRIATE TOPIC

The purpose of these essays is to let admissions get to know you, but if you are wondering if a certain topic is taboo, check in with a school counselor or other trusted adult. Potentially difficult topics include suicide, rape, criminal behavior, abusive parents, and drug abuse. Sometimes, how you handle or approach the topic makes the difference between taboo and acceptable. You would certainly want to show a positive outcome or growth and how you got there. A good rule of thumb is the "too much information" test: If someone winces and says, "TMI!" when you discuss this topic, don't go there in your essay. In all but one situation, I have advised my students to stay clear of difficult subjects for the simple reason that they had stronger topics to explore.

DIVERSITY PROMPTS

Diversity. This is one of those words you should look up so you completely understand it. *Diversity* goes beyond race or religion and whether or not you belong to a minority group. Schools with these prompts are basically telling you they take pride in being a melting pot. They want to know what you will bring to their mix—not only via your personal diversity but your attitude toward others.

The Duke University diversity prompt does a good job of explaining:

PROMPT

Duke University seeks a talented, engaged student body that embodies the wide range of human experience; we believe that the diversity of our students makes our community stronger. If you'd like to share a perspective you bring or experiences you've had to help us understand you better—perhaps related to a community you belong to, your sexual orientation or gender identity, or your family or cultural background—we encourage you to do so. Real people are reading your application, and we want to do our best to understand and appreciate the real people applying to Duke.

This prompt makes it clear that *diversity* includes many aspects. Perhaps you have physical characteristics (hearing or vision impaired) or capabilities (bilingual) or maybe a situation (a Jewish kid attending a Catholic school, the only girl in the engineering club or guy in dance class) that sets you apart in some special way. Maybe you are on the autism spectrum. Or maybe you aren't on the spectrum, but your brother is, and this life experience has provided a level of patience, tolerance, and understanding that would benefit the school. Are you a white male? Don't shy away from a diversity prompt. You, too, are "real"; determine your unique perspective and express it.

Have something you need to hide from a certain school to get in? Suspect you'll feel uncomfortable in the campus culture? Don't apply! If you have no choice in the matter,

21

try to convince your parents that there are plenty of other good schools that will celebrate you just the way you are.

Some schools go beyond discussing diversity in general and ask students to relate it to a planned course of study or career. The California Institute of Technology has a diversity prompt like this:

PROMPT

In an increasingly global and interdependent society, there is a need for diversity in thought, background, and experience in science, technology, engineering, and mathematics. How do you see yourself contributing to the diversity of Caltech's community? [200 words]

Here's a sample response:

I grew up in urban Taipei, and while my family practices Buddhism, which helps me stay calm whenever I am stressed, the Taiwanese culture of Confucianism has taught me discipline and diligence. We moved to suburban San Diego before I started seventh grade, where American culture introduced me to creativity and teamwork. Having been exposed to American, Chinese, Japanese, New Zealander, and Australian people in Taiwan and the United States has made me open-minded toward others and their customs.

In addition to bringing my multicultural background to Caltech, I also bring my range of experiences in science. I have participated in two internships. At UCSD, I used microscopes to take pictures of tissues and cells to identify tumors. At Cornell, I learned how to perform mouse necropsies, process the organs, use a microtome to section organs, and stain tissues with markers. Previously, I took a biotechnology class at Brown where I learned how to use lab equipment such as micropipettes and perform procedures such as sterilization. Working with lab groups has taught me that teamwork not only decreases errors and expands conclusions drawn, but also helps me better understand procedures and provides the team with ideas to improve the next experiment.

THE DREADED "WHY" PROMPTS

"Why this school?" or "why this major?" prompts are most challenging. Why? They seem to have no room for creativity, especially when the word count is often limited to 100 or 250 words. Be wary of making statements instead of impressions, and avoid generic comments, including "top-ranked program," "low student-to-faculty ratio," "interdisciplinary studies," and "great alumni network."

Here's MIT's "why" prompt and a sample first draft:

PROMPT

Although you may not yet know what you want
to major in, which department or program at
MIT appeals to you and why? (100 words)

I've always enjoyed my friends at Math Club, whether
we're tinkering with projects or challenging each
other to solve tricky AIME* problems. These guys
have always made me feel welcome, even though I'm
one of the few girls. I look forward to working with
similar people in the CSAIL* program.

We know this student likes math, but we don't learn
much else about her; she didn't tailor this essay to the specific university, either. She could submit this exact same
essay to another school by merely changing the name of
the academic program, not to mention that one of the other
girls in Math Club could submit the same essay. The student doesn't present as special—yet!—nor has she shown
the school to which she is applying that it is special, too. I
asked her to do some free-form writing on why she liked
computer science and engineering. After brainstorming,
she culled material to color her essay. She also did further

---

* *American Invitational Mathematics Examinations, Computer Science and Artificial Intelligence Laboratory. In this situation, the target reader will know the abbreviations, so it's not worth wasting precious characters spelling them out.*

> On a poster in my room, a UFO hovers above the words, "I want to believe." I chose MIT EECS* because I want to believe in the bizarre and unimagined, much like what inspired MIT EECS senior John Romanishin. Perhaps his self-assembling robots, which overturned conventional models of modular robotics, will open doors to many real-life applications. He didn't listen to the people who told him it couldn't be done. At MIT, I hope to follow CSAIL professors like David Karger and Daniela Rus through UROP* and have the flexibility Romanishin had to indulge in projects and create something big.

In the revision, the student doesn't need to *tell* us she likes math and science—her writing makes it obvious. Also, this essay no longer works for one of her female buddies in Math Club, because the elements of exposition, such as the poster on the bedroom wall, are unique to her. We feel passion for her chosen field of study through phrases such as "I want to believe in the bizarre and unimagined." And finally, the student can no longer

---

* *Electrical Engineering and Computer Science, Undergraduate Research Opportunities Program. As earlier, this essay was going to MIT, where the readers will know the acronyms.*

submit this essay to another school. She has shown MIT she is sincerely interested because she has named specific MIT programs and people and related them to her goals. Take a moment and list all of the things you learned about this student in *one* paragraph!

As with the other prompts, be clear about what a "why" prompt is asking. I've removed the actual school names so you can easily see how these four prompts differ:

- Why State University?
- Why are you drawn to the area(s) of study indicated in your application?
- Describe the unique qualities that attract you to the specific undergraduate college or school to which you are applying at State University.
- How does State University, as you know it now, satisfy your desire for a particular kind of learning, community, and future? Please address with some specificity your own wishes and how they relate to State University.

The first school's prompt is wide open. Not only should you discuss academic opportunities available but you can also include campus clubs and events, school traditions, and the institution's surrounding community or city. Don't randomly throw stuff into your essay or it will be clear you lifted information from the school's website.

Anything included must have context and be relevant to you. Be genuine.

The second and third prompts, though similar, are slightly different. The second one's focus is "area(s) of study," while the third's is a "specific undergraduate college or school." The latter is slightly broader. "Why are you drawn to" and "describe the unique qualities that attract you" are also similar, but you'll need to tweak your responses to satisfy the specific prompt.

The fourth prompt is similar to the first but goes into more detail explaining the prompt and asks you to specifically address three things: learning, community, and future.

With any prompt, do your homework about the specific school. Have you visited or will you visit the school? When you do, take a guided tour, talk with students, try to meet with professors and students in your major, and take notes! If you can't visit the school, investigate the school's website, talk to any friends or acquaintances who go there, or contact alumni in your area. Get school-specific information as it relates to you and the prompt. In these "why" essays, be prepared to mention a faculty member you'd like to study or work with—and give explanations. If applicable, mention specific research conducted at the school, any internship or program opportunities that interest you, and reasons for their appeal.

Here is one student's "why" essay for two different schools:

PROMPT

What in particular about Yale has influenced
your decision to apply? [100 words]

As I want to pursue a career in cancer research, I'd like to get involved with the Yale Cancer Prevention and Control Program and learn more about Professor Tish Knobf's research on interventions to enhance outcomes for women diagnosed with and surviving cancer. I'm also interested in Professor Dennis Cooper's work with stem cell transplants in the treatment of breast cancer. I learn best by experiencing and experimenting, so I hope to further my laboratory research experience by participating in the STARS I Summer Program. I would also like to join Undergraduate Women in Science to support women in STEM.

PROMPT

Although you may not yet know what you want
to major in, which department or program at
MIT appeals to you and why? [100 words]

After my internship in cancer research last summer, I decided to major in Biology/Course 7, focusing on cell, developmental, and molecular biology. I would love to learn more about Professor Jacqueline Lees' research on protein pathways and their role in tumorigenicity using zebrafish. I'm interested to see how proteins mediate control of the cell cycle to suppress tumors. The Undergraduate Research Opportunities Program also interests me because I learn better through doing, experimenting, and experiencing. Specifically, I would like to participate in Professor Michael Hemann's study on the mechanisms by which tumors resist chemotherapy treatment.

The student had to do a lot of research even for a one-paragraph essay, but that's what it takes to convince a school you are a serious contender.

Many students have not nailed down a major or a career goal when they enter college, and this is OK (not for graduate school applications, however). What is important: that you can define areas of interest to show admissions you have some direction. That said, don't apply to a tech school if you don't have any interest in the sciences, and don't apply to an agricultural school if you think you want to work in psychology or marketing.

Don't get sloppy with these "why" essays; be aware of each school as you write. If you refer to a popular place on campus or the school's colors, be sure you've got such details right! I had one student rejected because he emailed admissions about a swim team the school didn't have.

SIMILAR PROMPTS

Some prompts are similar, but rarely, if ever, can you simply copy an essay from one school to another. Learn to recognize each prompt's subtle differences. Highlighting key words and listing prompts points is a good way to do this.

PROMPT

Caltech students have long been known for their quirky sense of humor, whether it be through planning creative pranks, building elaborate party sets, or even the year-long preparation that goes in our annual Ditch Day. Please describe an unusual way in which you have fun.

Caltech owns its quirkiness, and the key word here is "unusual." Make sure that your way of having fun is unusual (also make sure it is legal and does not harm people or other living things!).

Across the country at MIT, you'll find this prompt:

PROMPT

We know you lead a busy life, full of activities, many of which are required of you. Tell us about something you do simply for the pleasure of it.

Students who apply to Caltech often apply to MIT, and vice versa. While you could submit a shortened version of your Caltech essay to MIT (the latter has a lower word count), you could not submit your MIT essay to Caltech unless that thing you do simply for the *pleasure* of it is also *unusual*.

LIST PROMPTS

Some prompts ask you to list things. Here are a few examples, all of which concern books:

- List five books you have read in the past two years.
- Please list three books, along with their authors, that have been particularly meaningful to you. For each book, please include a sentence explaining their influence upon you. Please note that your response is not limited to math, science or school-assigned texts.
- Share with us a few of your favorite books, poems, authors, films, plays, pieces of music, musicians, performers, paintings, artists, blogs, magazines or newspapers. Feel free to touch on one, some, or all of the categories listed, or add a category of your own.

With the first prompt, all your response needs is a list of the books. The key word in the second prompt is "meaningful," and though this prompt is for a science and technology school, the prompt is clear that the books' subjects can be about anything. To me, this prompt is hinting that the school is interested in more than students who are science whizzes; they want *well-rounded* science whizzes. The third prompt is similar to the first one, except it goes beyond books. But note time differences: the first prompt is concerned with the last *two years*, while the third asks for your *favorites*.

Here's another example of a list prompt:

PROMPT

List five adjectives that best describe you.

Start by making your own list. Be authentic. Then, ask your parents, some friends, and a respected teacher or coach to describe you. Do any patterns emerge? Those are probably the keepers, unless you have words with similar meaning.

Here's what one student started with:

Empathetic, articulate, leader, candid, sassy, kind, gregarious, ambitious, intuitive, intelligent.

"Empathetic" and "kind" are in the same ballpark. "Intuitive" and "intelligent" are also related, but "intuitive" goes deeper, and when we say it about ourselves, "intelligent" can come across as bragging. "Intelligent" is also built into "intuitive." "Sassy" was a definite keeper;

the student chose to list it last because it served as an exclamation point and sounded best there. The student was left with these words:

Articulate, leader, candid, kind, gregarious, ambitious, intuitive, sassy.

To narrow down, I suggested the student ask herself which five adjectives would present the broadest picture of herself and, in combination, would make her sound most interesting. Here is her final list:

Kind, intuitive, gregarious, candid, sassy.

If the prompt says "list," then that's all you do. If it leaves room via word count to elaborate or asks you to do so, here is an example of how you can make a list a little more exciting:

PROMPT

What were your favorite events (e.g., performances, exhibits, competitions, conferences, etc.) in recent years? (50 words)

My favorite events were the Grossology Exhibit at the Reuben H. Fleet Science Center, 2014 Oscars, Idina Menzel's "Barefoot at the Symphony" concert, University of Toronto National Biology Competition, San

Antonio's defeat of Miami in Game 5 of the 2014 NBA Championships, and eating pho with friends after AP testing.

ANOTHER EXAMPLE—

The "All that Glitters" gemstone exhibit at Balboa Park (especially the watermelon tourmaline); listening to the biomedical companies and researchers present their discoveries at the BIO Convention in San Diego; and being part of the amazing crowd energy at the professional League of Legends tournament at the Los Angeles Staples Center.

PROMPT

Tell us where you have lived—and for how long—since you were born; whether you've always lived in the same place, or perhaps in a variety of places. (100 words)

This prompt does not tell you to list, but you have only one hundred words. Still, you can infuse some personality.

Nine houses, six cities, and three countries. My father's job as a hotel manager caused my family to move around a lot. I was born in Taipei, and resided there until moving to the San Francisco suburb of Foster City for kindergarten. Next stop was a 26th-floor-apartment in the heart of busting Beijing, then the Park Hyatt. Fifth grade brought a dramatic change of pace when we moved to the more rural city of Guangzhou. After eighth grade in urban Shanghai, my father finally retired, and we settled down again in the Bay Area, this time in Palo Alto.

Don't worry if you have lived in only one city or one house your entire life. If you have the word count, amplify the bare facts a little so we get a clear picture of where you come from.

OPTIONAL PROMPTS

Answer them! If you don't, you are basically telling the school you have better things to do with your time (such as work on the optional essay for your preferred school). Of course, if the optional prompts do not apply to you— for example, a prompt asks you to discuss a physical handicap or learning disability and how you have managed it—move on.

INTERNATIONAL STUDENTS

If English is your second language, be sure to discuss the prompt with a native speaker. I've had international students who, although fluent in English, still misunderstood nuances of certain prompts. If you learn this after you have already brainstormed and crafted a first draft, you have wasted a lot of time.

WHEN YOU HAVE OPTIONS

When faced with choosing one prompt from a group (as with the Common App) or several from a group (as with UC), go with the one(s) you feel drawn to. If you aren't sure, start by eliminating the prompts that don't excite you at all. Unfortunately, some schools leave you no choice. If you are struggling with a required prompt, try changing your angle of approach. This may help you find ways to emotionally connect with the prompt.

The Common App and some schools give you the option to create your own topic. If you go this route, be sure to delineate your prompt so you keep your focus when writing. And keep in mind the goal of these essays: to reveal to admissions who you are.

When selecting topics for a package of essays for one school, some strategizing occurs (we'll discuss this later).

3

THE DETAILS

There's a famous Wendy's commercial from 1984 (view it on YouTube) wherein three elderly women peering over a fast food counter inspect a huge, fluffy hamburger bun on a plate. When one of them lifts the top to reveal a tee-ny-weeny burger, another cries:

> Where's the beef?!

An essay that is all fluff and no beef will not satisfy admissions. The beef is in the details, and it is through these details that total strangers will connect with your writing . . . and you. The noted psychologist and author Carl R. Rogers said:

What is most personal is most universal.

I've heard iterations of this quote in writing workshops, and it is so true. Back in 1972, when television was in its toddler years and I was a kid, ABC telecast the Munich Olympics. Typical sports coverage of the era consisted of merely pointing cameras at competitors and reporting results, but the ABC team went beyond, bringing viewers "the human drama of athletic competition." And they did so by inaugurating what would become a staple in sports television: "Up Close and Personal" segments. These video personality profiles gave viewers a look into the lives of American and international athletes. Learning their personal stories and what made them tick made us want to watch them compete. Imagine everyone in America knowing a 350-pound Soviet weightlifter by name in the midst of the Cold War . . . and tuning in to cheer him on! That's right, a Soviet weightlifter! And I can still tell you his name decades later (Vasily Alekseyev). Why? Because knowing the details of his life story made me care.

Details in your writing will do the same. They will enable complete strangers in the admissions office to connect with and care about you. When do we give up on a book or change the channel or walk out of a movie? When we don't care about the people on the pages or the screen.

. . . For extra credit, I opted to attend a "Take Back the Night" event that was preceded by a march against sexual assault. I had never participated in a march before. Nervously, I picked up a sign and mimed the chants as we paraded around campus. My silence eventually turned to whispers and then to shouting. Tears of absolution flooded in as I defended a cause that had silently been my own.

This passage from a prospective graduate student's personal statement wasn't bad at all, but I wanted to know more. "What were you chanting?" I asked the student. "And what exactly were you holding in?" The next draft came back like this:

. . . I opted to attend a "Take Back the Night" event for extra credit. The event was preceded by a march against sexual assault. I had never participated in a march before. I nervously picked up a sign, unaware of what it said, and mimed the chant "2, 4, 6, 8, Stop the violence! Stop the rape!" as we paraded around campus. "Stop the violence! Stop the Rape!" Tears of absolution flooded in as I defended a cause that had silently been my own.

The added details raise the passage's level of intensity and emotion. We can see the writer shouting, and we now understand why. Her story grabs us.

ASSUME YOUR READER KNOWS NOTHING

Writers are often so close to the person or subject matter they are writing about they forget to include necessary details. We, your readers, come to your writing dumb and blind. We don't know about your world, and we have never seen it. So, whether your essay topic is a person, a thing, or a place, you must clue us in. Pull us into your world. And the way you do that is by describing the necessary details.

Are you writing about your big brother?

- Remember, we have never met him.
- What do we need to know about him that is *relevant* to this essay?

Are you writing about a certain fencing match?

- Remember, we weren't there.
- We likely don't understand the protocol or terminology, either.

Are you writing about your summer spent doing medical research?

- Remember, we might not know anything about genomics.
- Write so we laypeople can understand.

Are you writing about the first time you visited Yosemite?

- Remember, we may not have been there.
- Even if we have, we need to see the place through *your* eyes.

THINK LIKE A REPORTER

Many first drafts are loaded with statements: "I like listening to classical music," "I want to study computer science," "My view on life in the United States has changed a lot." Statements are generic and colorless. To give writing life and make it unique, research and brainstorm as if you were a reporter.

Behind every statement is a plethora of details! Flesh them out by conducting yourself as a journalist: Ask questions and then ask follow-up questions. Rely on the Five Ws:

> Who, what, when, where, why . . . and how.

Classical music, for example, is a huge category. Apply those Five Ws to uncover details. Questions you might ask: *What* composer(s), period(s), style(s), or piece(s) in particular may be your favorites? *Why* do you like that particular composer, period, style or piece? *When* did your view on life in the United States change? *What* happened that changed your view? *How* did that event make you feel?

To generate even more details, you can also access the five senses:

[Smell, touch, taste, hearing, sight.]

Every essay may not need all Five *W*s or senses to generate details, but explore. As you start writing, what information is appropriate and will best serve your essay will be revealed.

Thinking like a reporter means that a statement such as this . . .

. . . It would mean that I could have opinions on which restaurant made the best sushi or who was the best action film director, but I could not say anything about issues that truly mattered.

can be transformed into a sentence like this:

. . . Apparently, my critique of the Spider Roll at Jin Sho Sushi was acceptable posting material, but I was not to discuss anything of true importance to me.

Small changes, such as incorporating the "what" and "where" details, make this statement more visual and humorous and, therefore, more memorable. We know more about the writer, and that gives her credibility.

[Actions speak louder than statements.]

Take a look at this student's writing:

There is no place where I feel more at home than in the comfort of my very own house, in front of the liquid crystal display that I like to call my laptop.

Throughout the first seventeen years of my life, I've participated in many activities—including piano, tennis, and math—and I have definitely enjoyed each of them. But hitting a ball with a racket for hundreds of times gets boring, as does mulling over Taylor Polynomials in a dormitory for hours on end. I've quite literally tried to stay interested in scales and arpeggios for lengthened periods of time, but that didn't work out very well, either . . .

Note the student *tells* us he has participated in many activities. Then, he lists them. Then, he *tells* us he enjoys them. These are statements. Yet his later comments about piano lessons, tennis drills, and math practice are much more interesting. Why? Because this writing is *descriptive*. When I asked the student to rewrite his piece, he deleted the list and statement because they were no longer needed.

I also asked him if he truly liked piano, tennis, and math (it didn't sound like it). Finally, I suggested he rearrange his thoughts in order to build drama. Here's how the paragraph changed:

> I love to play tennis, but drilling hundreds of cross-court forehands and backhands can get boring. Solving challenging math problems gives my mind a workout, but mulling over Taylor Polynomials for hours on end eventually gets tiresome. And while playing the piano often takes me away to a surreal world, practicing scales and arpeggios tends to wear on me after some time. However, when I settle back into my favorite chair, power on my laptop, and dive into the world beyond the liquid crystal display . . .

The actions described present information about the student with much more dazzle and emotion. The writing is also crisper because redundancies have been deleted (more on that later), so each sentence is now relating new information to the reader.

Go back and read that paragraph, and find the lingering statement. Yes, you could replace "I love to play tennis" with something like "I love the smack of the ball flying off the strings." So look for those spots in your writing where you can eliminate redundancies and replace statements with descriptive detail.

TELLING—

I am an amateur photographer.

SHOWING—

I strolled up and down the sand thinking I would take
some pictures with my DSLR.

TELLING—

My mom and aunt were preparing traditional Chinese
New Year foods.

SHOWING—

My eyes hungrily moved down the counter as the smell
of all the different foods hit me. Rice cakes, symbolic
of the Chinese character for improvement, were
stacked on top of each other; savory steamed fish,
symbolic of prosperity, was drizzled with soy sauce;
and next to that was an enormous plate of dumplings,
symbolic of wealth. Finally, my favorite: Aunt May's
delicious beef and rice dish, which she made for every
family gathering.

TELLING—

. . . I am not usually a provocative child. I am not a
rebel. I do have beliefs, values, ethics, opinions . . .
from this emerges my own system of rights and

wrongs that I have slowly fine-tuned as my collection of experiences has grown into a library, a museum even. I always want to speak out against that which I believe violates my system of rights and wrongs . . .

SHOWING—

. . . I am not usually a provocative child. I am not a rebel. But the day before, I had read a powerful letter on Facebook written by a woman who was raped on a college campus by a star swimmer. I was traumatized when I read how she "wanted to take off her skin like a jacket" and would never "get back [her] life from before that night." Her description of the callousness her attacker showed at the trial by blaming their intoxication made me furious, as did the listing of his swim times at the end of the article. This woman's story also made me anxious—I was only a year away from going to college, where statistics show that one out of every five female students will be sexually assaulted. I prayed that I would not become another "unconscious intoxicated woman," as one newspaper had described the victim.

My eyes stared blankly at the small screen in my palm, my thumb tapping the impassive surface. I pressed "share" . . .

Any time you feel stuck in series of statements, channel your three-year-old self. Toddlers never let anyone get away with a statement! "But why?" they ask. Small children are curious about everything they see or are asked to do, whether it's statements like "the sun doesn't shine at night" or instructions, such as "put your shoes on." And they will relentlessly follow any adult's response with at least two more "but whys?!"

WATCH YOUR LANGUAGE

Whether the subject is smashing of protons or rhythmic gymnastics, that interest or hobby will have its own terminology. Remember to write so that someone completely unfamiliar with the topic can get pulled in and follow along. Think of some of your favorite movies, especially if they take place in a time or galaxy far, far away. These worlds are completely unfamiliar, but good writing pulls you into the story.

PROMPT

Some students have a background, identity, interest, or talent that is so meaningful they believe their application would be incomplete without it. If this sounds like you, then please share your story. (300-500 words)

The non-stop CLICK CLICK of pens is making my head spin—I can't concentrate on the number theory problem before me. Everything I write down is immediately scribbled out. No good. I've tried everything: Chinese Remainder Theorem, Lifting the Exponent . . . 1:14.55 remaining. Where did the last eight minutes go?

Wait . . . if I square both sides an infinite amount of times, couldn't I just condense the values into an integral? Or will it just be a lengthy Taylor Series? No time to think. Go! . . .

Whether in a competitive or academic arena, math has made my life more exciting. Trips around the world; the intense, brain-frying problem sets; the dynamic teamwork challenges; the delectable combination of stress and satisfaction in a fierce contest; and the application of a dynamic subject to the real world—math has changed the way I look at everything . . .

I have no idea what the Chinese Remainder Theorem is (or, for that matter, Lifting the Exponent). Still, this essay works because there is enough context for me to connect the dots. The simplest way to test an essay with technical jargon is to have someone who is unfamiliar with your topic read it. Now, consider your audience. If you are addressing a reader who speaks your language (for example, you are writing a required supplemental essay for a specific department or concentration), then you don't need to explain everything.

HAVE NO FEAR

> If you're afraid of who you are,
> your writing will reflect that.
> Be brave and your words will spark to flame.

I heard these words of wisdom from a teenager at a writing workshop. Bottom line: If you don't reveal something about yourself, your writing will be bland, and you will not stand out in the crowd of applicants. If necessary, create a safe space so your writing can be daring and honest. For some, that may mean asking your parents to not hover while you go through this process and to wait to see your essays until you are ready to share them.

I'll never forget when I sat down with one student to review her first draft for the following University of Pennsylvania essay:

PROMPT

Ben Franklin once said, "All mankind is divided into three classes: those that are immovable, those that are movable, and those that move." Which are you? [300-500 words]

The student decided that, depending on the situation, she fit into all three. Here's how she described her immovable side:

On rare occasions, I am immovable. On the first day of chemistry class, my teacher, Ms. Smith, listed every single lab rule to the class, stressing the importance of wearing protective clothing, keeping chemicals away from the face, and following directions. Every procedure is crucial to completing a lab report. After the first two or three experiments, many students began to skip a few steps to finish the experiments more quickly. I, however, continued to follow each step, one by one. Some classmates called me foolish; others called me stubborn. But I never changed my mind. I knew that in a serious research experiment, skipping a single step cannot only alter the results, but could also be a fatal mistake. Just as in hospitals, where diseases and viruses collect, a single mistake such as mislabeling or forgetting to sanitize instruments, can lead to a serious, unfixable mistake. I believe there are some principles that must be fully looked into, even if this process will delay a situation. To what I believe is right, I am immovable.

My first reaction was that the student was forcing the essay when, about halfway through the paragraph, she made statements that seemed intended to prove she would make a good medical practitioner (which was her career goal). She also strayed from describing herself—and addressing the prompt—to write extensively about something that didn't seem to warrant such attention, especially considering the word limit. Most importantly, I sensed she was playing it safe, perhaps because she knew her parents would ultimately read her essay. (Did I mention that her mother was also sitting in the room?) I reminded the student that I was in high school once and had experienced my share of peer pressure. "What is *really* going on around you?" I asked. And then her truth came out. Here's what the paragraph looked like in the end:

Occasionally, I am immovable. On the first day of chemistry class during my junior year, my teacher wrote a list of every single lab rule to the class, stressing the importance of wearing protective clothing, keeping chemicals away from the face, and following directions. She further emphasized that each procedure was crucial to completing a lab report. After two or three experiments, many students began to skip a few steps in order to finish more quickly. I, however, continued to follow each step, one by one. Some classmates called me foolish; others called me stubborn. But I never changed my mind. Likewise, throughout my junior year, some friends began using prescription stimulants, intended to ease symptoms of ADHD, to concentrate when studying or taking a test. It turned into a trend. Whether the drug was falsely prescribed for my friends or shared among them, more and more students began taking it to improve their grades and get through their difficult classes. When a friend offered some pills to me, I rejected them, even though I had a huge English final coming up. Just as skipping a single step in a research experiment or surgical procedure can lead to a fatal, irrevocable mistake, I knew that taking the drug, even once, could have the same result. I didn't want to look back one day and regret this decision. When I feel like my beliefs are being challenged, I am immovable.

This version is cohesive because the student ties her thoughts together. It feels more genuine and reveals much more about her character and belief system.

Side note: One could argue that the student was trying to be unique or clever by saying she was all three attributes (immovable, movable, and moves), but this essay was successful because it was her truth.

CAN YOU PASS YOUR ESSAY TO THE RIGHT?

Let's say you, the second chair violin of your high school orchestra, are applying to a music program. Your best friend, the concertmaster, also plans to attend that school. If you passed your "why are you applying to this program" essay to your right, could your friend also submit it? If the answer is yes, then you haven't written a personal essay; you've spent 250 to 650 words transforming your resume into prose and making generic statements. Boring!

Hundreds of violinists will be applying to that program, just as innumerable pre-med students will be applying to the biology program, and so on. This does not mean that musicians can't write about their interest unless they play some exotic instrument, like an agung a tamlang or a balafon. It's OK if you play the common violin, but you must relate your *personal* experience with it.

PROMPT

We know you lead a busy life, full of activities, many of which are required of you. Tell us about something you do for the pleasure of it. (100 words)

When I play the violin, I feel liberated. I'm particularly drawn to Bach's music even though it has complicated rhythms, a solid Baroque structure, and lines woven within harmonic chords. That doesn't sound very liberating, but as violinist Hilary Hahn said about Bach's music, "Sometimes the most mathematical seeming music is the most liberating to play." When I play a piece like Sonata No. 2, Grave, I am able to stretch and pull the rhythms and shape phrases out of the notes. As I dig into my own creativity, I feel at peace and content with myself.

Only this student could submit this essay; it is uniquely hers. The details also tell us more than the fact that she plays the violin for pleasure. In a mere one hundred words, we also learn that she enjoys Bach's music, and has a deep understanding of music—and a playful sense of language.

Here's the start of another violinist's essay for a similar prompt:

When my fingers dance across the ebony hardwood, the vibrations of the strings tickle my fingertips, and harmonious chords ring through the air. I find joy in being able to bring the ink on the page to life, to find spiritual peace in the creations of Bach, to channel Tchaikovsky's deep suffering, and to entertain others and myself with the skillful musical quips of Saint-Saëns . . .

Both of these students likely started with the tip of the iceberg (i.e., "I like to play the violin") when they began brainstorming, but by going below the surface, they found their unique expression of the same passion.

To find your story, do your thing. Whatever that is, have your laptop or a notepad nearby. If you're a cook, go make a mess in the kitchen! If you're a skier, take that favorite run! If you're a mad scientist, extract that DNA! Whatever your thing is, do it while being hyper aware and in tune with your senses. Take notes. Then, write about all those sensations and emotions.

These details—the hallmark of good storytelling—will

help you paint literary pictures of yourself, the people in your life, and your experiences. If readers can walk into your world and see, taste, smell, and touch it, you have done your job . . . and admissions will sit up and notice.

4

CRAFTING

Once you have completely investigated your topic and exhausted your thoughts brainstorming, it's time to start putting your essay together.

HINT

Work on one essay at a time. You are going to get better at writing and understanding this process as you go. By focusing, you will save yourself a lot of time and frustration.

Before going any further, look at your notes. Are they all in one giant, overwhelming run-on paragraph? If so, you won't know where to start.

DIVIDE AND CONQUER

If you brainstormed on a computer, go back and insert paragraph breaks between distinct thoughts and points. As you do this, you might find that some items near the end of your notes tie in with other things written earlier. Move sentences and paragraphs around until similar thoughts are clumped together. Don't worry about order or flow or grammar or anything making total sense; for now, you are simply sorting data. If you are a more visual person, try using a graphic organizer. (See an example in the Appendix.)

If you did your brainstorming on paper, type your notes into the computer and go through the previous exercise. Having a printed version of your notes will make them easier to review and refer to as you craft your essay.

Now, print your notes on good old-fashioned paper so you can get physical with what you've written. Wade into your rivers of words and pan for the gold. Highlight what sparkles to you—anything that seems interesting or "good." These nuggets and flecks will become the bones and content of your essay. Even though they are currently raw and unrefined, they will morph as you work through the writing process.

> Don't expect perfection on the
> first draft —or the second one, either!

The creative process is called a process for a reason. Michelangelo said this about sculpting: "The idea is there locked inside. All you have to do is remove the excess stone." And so it is with writing. Your slab of marble is that white page or screen in front of you, and as that page fills with words, you will see the form emerging. Don't fret if all you observe at first is a hand, because that hand wants to get free. As you chip away the excess stone, that hand will lead you to an arm, which will then lead you to a torso, and before long, you will literally see your creation appearing. When it does, you will know exactly what to do with it.

My writing motto:

[Exposition first. Form later.]

I know, I know; this sounds as if I just told you to forget everything you learned in English composition! Ultimately, you will find order and structure—I'm simply suggesting a different way of getting there. Release yourself from the shackles of outlining, devising topic sentences, and overplanning, which only stifles creativity and voice. Trust me: Your essay will find its form. For now, loosen up so you can be playful and discover.

KEEP THE PROMPT IN FRONT OF YOU

Literally! Before you write a word, type the prompt at the top of the page. Add the word count and your list of points. Refer to these items often. You may write a fabulous essay, but if it doesn't address the prompt, you have thrown an air ball. If you are working with a teacher, counselor, or writing coach, keep the prompt and word count at the top of the drafts you send for review. You need to write to the prompt, and your advisers need to be able to edit to it.

> You don't have to "answer" or restate the prompt in the first sentence or opening paragraph.

PROMPT

What attribute of your personality are you most proud of, and how has it impacted your life so far? This could be your creativity, effective leadership, sense of humor, integrity, or anything else you'd like to tell us about. (200–250 words)

I was kicked out of the soup kitchen because I was ten minutes late for my shift. As I drove down the street, searching for somewhere else I could spend my Saturday morning, I saw that spot of blue on my GPS. That was where I wanted to go: the beach.

I strolled up and down the sand thinking I would take some pictures with my DSLR, but I got distracted watching the dolphins play in the waves behind the surfers. That was when a man with crazy long white hair came up to me. We started talking, and he commented that I had a "romance" with surfing. He was right; I had always wanted to learn. As we walked, he greeted his many friends and then took me to the surf shop. Turns out he owned it. When I left an hour later, I had a new job.

I loved my experience last summer. I made new friends and became part of a new world. I learned that, despite what my parents taught me, it's okay to wander when I feel safe, it's okay to talk to strangers, and it's okay to try something new. As I enter college, I know that that adventurous side of me will not only open many roads but also enable me to keep up with computer science, a field that is constantly evolving. Whichever roads I choose to take, I'm confident that, as long as I follow through, they will lead me somewhere.

If this essay opened with "I am most proud of my adventurous side," it wouldn't be nearly as engaging to read. This was, of course, the first thing the student wrote on the page while brainstorming because she couldn't write about the attribute until she identified it. But that didn't mean that's where her essay ultimately had to start. Instead, the writer opted to tell a story, causing the reader to wonder where it would go. And there is nothing like getting your reader's attention in the first sentence.

Once again, look at all the information this essay reveals about the student: she volunteers, she likes the beach, she is a photographer, she is social, she likes surfing, she has had a job, she is adventurous. But none of these points are made as statements; they come out through a story that runs right on the spine of the prompt. And because this student's attributes are revealed through story, they don't sound like bragging.

ADDRESS THE KEY WORDS AND PHRASES

While you don't have to restate or answer the prompt verbatim, your essay should touch on the key words and phrases. In this example prompt, these key elements are "attribute," "most proud of," and "impacted your life." You don't have to incorporate all of these elements; use whatever feels right in your essay. Notice this student didn't use *any* key words/phrases; she opted instead to employ synonyms and related phrases, such as "that adventurous side of me" and "I loved my experience." And she didn't have to *tell* us about the impact of her attribute in her life. She conveyed it through story: She landed a new job and knows that following her sense of adventure will always lead her somewhere.

READY? GO!

Refer to your highlights and start writing. Don't judge yourself; just keep going, because the more words you get on the paper or screen, the more they will tell you what to do with your essay. Let the magic happen.

If you're feeling overwhelmed, cut up your thoughts. A laptop screen is small, and most cannot fully display an entire readable page. So physically print those words on paper and then use scissors to separate ideas. Try arranging those thoughts in one order, then slide the pieces of paper around in new patterns. Keep switching things up until you sense you're onto something. Once you "see" your essay, or even part of it, start writing.

You can also employ this "divide and conquer" method later in your writing process if you feel as if your essay isn't flowing.

Once you have your first draft, congratulations! The fun is about to begin, because good writing is all about rewriting.

5

PRE-EDITING CHECKLIST

Before you spend any more of your precious time editing and polishing, check the following items.

HAVE YOU ADDRESSED THE PROMPT?

This might seem obvious, but wandering from the prompt is a common error.

PROMPT

Every person has a creative side, and it can be expressed in many ways: problem solving, original and innovative thinking, and artistically, to name a few. Describe how you express your creative side. (350 words)

Onions. What a versatile food! While you may not think much of the layered, bulbous vegetable, it is one of the most important ingredients in my kitchen. It can be sweet, when sautéed with butter, as the base under perfectly seared scallops. It can be spicy, like in a mango salsa, giving a dish the kick it needs. Or, it can be a neutralizing agent, balancing out the sharp taste of capers on a beef carpaccio. The identity of the ingredient changes, depending on what other ingredients it is paired with. To me, cooking is like being a choreographer, and I am creating a dance between the different ingredients. I can use different methods of cooking to bring out the star in each show. If I dice the onion, it will have a sharper taste than if I fry it, or a much sweeter taste if I grill it . . .

If we hadn't read the prompt, we'd think that this essay is about the versatile onion! There was a diamond in the rough draft here, though, with the dancing metaphor. I suggested to the student that she run with that and pull the focus back to her creative expression as a cook (you can read her final essay in the Appendix).

<hr>

PROMPT

Virtually all of Stanford's undergraduates live on campus. Write a note to your future roommate that reveals something about you or that will help your roommate—and us—know you better.

<hr>

One of my students wrote a perfectly decent first draft for this prompt, but he left out one critical element: He neglected to address his roommate!

HAVE YOU RESPONDED TO EACH POINT IN THE PROMPT?

Read through your essay, and check off each point in your list as you address it. Are you giving each point equal or appropriate weight in your essay? In other words, if you have a three-point prompt and a three-paragraph essay and you spent two of those paragraphs on only one point, you need to cut down those two paragraphs and build up the other two points. That said, you might not need a separate paragraph for each point. Regardless of how you piece together your thoughts, you should give equal or appropriate weight to each point.

Early drafts are often overweight in the background or set-up paragraphs. If any of your background detail is running long, condense it. You are not writing a novel and must meet word count, so cut to the chase.

HAVE YOU STAYED ON TOPIC?

Screenwriters, unlike novelists, are limited by time. Therefore, every action and line of dialogue must be a necessity in moving the plot forward. Likewise, in essays with short word counts, every sentence must stay on the spine of the prompt. It's easy to stray when writing about someone who influenced you, an extracurricular activity, your favorite class in school, or a "why" prompt.

- If you've written about a book that has changed your life, but your essay is a summary of *Zen and the Art of Motorcycle Maintenance* that doesn't specifically share how this book has impacted your photography hobby (and you have explained those details), then your essay is not at full throttle.

- If you've written about being a member of the golf team (your favorite extracurricular activity), but all you talk about is the sport and your team's accomplishments, your essay is not up to par.

Of course, in these examples, you would need to briefly describe the book or the activity, but don't devote your entire essay to this. Look to nuances in the prompt for guidance: "Why is this activity *important* to you" or "What did you *contribute*."

"Why" prompts bring up similar issues:

- If, for example, you've gone into great detail about the engineering department at a certain school, but you neglected to tell us *why* a specific discipline, track, professor, research topic, or internship is relevant to *you* and *your future*, then the essay is not structurally sound.

I can't say this enough: Keep that prompt in front of you, and remember that the ultimate purpose of these essays is to give the admissions committee as much insight as possible into *you*—not Ben Franklin or a favorite subject or some hobby. Weigh the elements of your essay. If you have placed too much emphasis on your topic, cut what isn't relevant and circle back to *you*.

6

EDITING BASICS

Writing truly begins at the editing phase. There are now enough words on paper that they literally tell you what is needed ... and what isn't. Good editing, like good writing, takes more than one pass because each time you make a change, *everything* changes. These next few chapters include some tips to help you recognize that "excess stone," a.k.a the dull and useless bits. With practice, you'll get better at editing.

THE DOMINO THEORY OF EDITING

If you have a set of dominoes in the house (mahjong tiles will also suffice), go get it. On your desk or the floor, assemble standing tiles to form a snake so that if you were to trip the first tile, they would all fall down in a chain reaction. Remove a tile. This creates a small space; if you were to trip the first tile now, all the rest would still likely fall. But if you were to pull several tiles, the resulting gap would leave part of your snake still standing. To accommodate for those changes and have all the tiles fall, you would need to rearrange or add tiles. In those places where you added tiles, you might need more room, which means you might need to increase the arc of a curve.

Think of this snake as your essay. Each tile represents parts of your essay—words, sentences, or paragraphs—that have been strung together. Like writing, editing is a process. With each editing pass, you will pull what you don't need, move some things to other positions, or add new material. Change one word, and you may need to change the entire sentence. Change a sentence, and you may need to alter the one before it. And after it. And then the entire paragraph. Change a paragraph . . . You get the idea. You must consider how changes made affect the *entire* essay. As you look at each fresh configuration, things often come to light that you didn't notice or consider on a previous pass.

You want to enter each essay, paragraph, and sentence as late as possible and exit as early as possible. Remove as many "tiles" as you can while allowing those that remain to still trip seamlessly.

VISUAL IMPRESSIONS

You turn the page of a book only to encounter a daunting paragraph that fills the entire sheet. No white space is anywhere in sight. Do you want to read it? No!

When writing, think like a gourmet chef. That culinary artist is just as interested in how she plates a meal as in how she prepares it. Presentation is key, as the eyes see the food *before* the tongue tastes it. Similarly, the eyes *see* your essay before reading it. Paragraph breaks will make your essay visually inviting and get your reader off to a good start. It also signals that you didn't simply slap your essay together and submit.

TENSE AND POINT OF VIEW

Consistency in tense and point of view is important to your essay. By nature, just about all college application essays are written in first person. They are also usually written in present tense, unless the writer is relating a story in the past. A great way to check your tense is to circle all the verbs. I see a lot of first drafts where the student writes about something in the past but uses present tense to create a sense of immediacy. When this doesn't work, the writing sounds affected. The chosen tense must fit within the context of the particular essay. Read your prompt out loud, then your essay. Does the tense sound natural? If so, go with it.

Also check that you maintain a consistent point of

view throughout the essay. I think the easiest way to understand point of view is to visualize it: Who is holding the camera in your piece, and where is it pointing? I have yet to encounter a college application essay that isn't written in first person ("I"), but I have seen writers stray into second person ("I" addresses "you") and third person (uninvolved narrator). If you start to sound like copy from the school's website or an article on your subject matter, you have likely lost sight of the most important element of your essay: *you* (see "Write Inside" for further discussion). If you deliberately attempt second person, make sure this device is serving you. I've had students directly address admissions, and when I read their work back to them, they could hear they sounded too cutesy, flippant, or arrogant.

FIRST PARAGRAPHS

James Bond movies are known for opening with 007 making a great escape, from skiing off a cliff in the Alps to BASE jumping from the top of a towering dam. These scenes pull us into the film in a matter of seconds. Now, not all essays can—or should—start with such a bolt of adrenaline, but do strive to make those opening sentences low-dangling, juicy fruit that your readers will want to bite into. Just be wary of trying too hard. Many of my students start their first drafts with a quote, almost all of which feel forced, inappropriate for the subject matter, or irrelevant.

> You don't have to open with a quote
> or an anecdote to be catchy.

Furthermore, if you do open all of your essays this way, your writing sounds contrived. Read your prompt out loud; then, read your first paragraph. Do your words feel like a natural response? Does the paragraph work? If it sounds concocted, try again.

Here's an example of a successful opening with a quote:

PROMPT

Reflect on a time when you challenged a belief or idea. What prompted you to act? Would you make the same decision again?

"Take that post off of Facebook!" my mother ordered. "You don't want to seem extremist." Extremist? I felt a tightness grow in my chest and took a deep breath, as if to build a dam to hold back the flood of emotions. "Girls should be likeable," she said, "and likeable girls don't have lots of opinions."

Does your opening sentence sound generic?

When I was six years old, my parents and I discovered that I had trouble hearing properly.

I asked the student, *how* did you discover that you had trouble hearing? The resulting sentence is much more interesting and visual:

> When I was six years old, my parents noticed that I would look at people's lips when they were talking instead of their eyes.

ANOTHER EXAMPLE—
As a freshman, I signed up to join my school's track team.

AFTER FISHING FOR A LITTLE MORE DETAIL—
My friend's eyes narrowed, looking at me with equal parts amusement and disbelief. "You? In track?" I knew what he meant—I looked like the type who'd rather fake a sprained ankle than run a lap or two in P.E.

These subtle changes bring forth distinctiveness and personality.

BURYING THE LEDE

Another first draft deficiency is what newspaper editors call "burying the lede." That's when the writer's best material, the stuff that piques a reader's interest and lays the foundation for what follows, is tucked somewhere in a later paragraph and needs to be moved downstage, front and center.

The following excerpt is from a personal statement for graduate studies in depth psychology with a specialization in community, liberation, and ecopsychology. Like most personal statements for graduate programs, the prompt is not detailed, but it is understood that the essay should include the typical "why" essay elements (including, why this school, program, degree, and track; career goals; what research being conducted is relevant; and relevant experience and personal background).

> Three years ago, I began psychotherapy with a therapist who utilizes the depth psychological approach. My journey into myself, drawing upon symbols and myth to interpret my psyche, reflected much of what I had read from one of my favorite minds: Joseph Campbell. The process has been wildly helpful. I have always found meaning in synchronistic idiosyncrasies. Paying attention to non-coincidental coincidences and following my intuition was rooted in reading books such as *The Celestine Prophecy* by James Redfield and Clarissa Pinkola Estes' *Women Who Run with the Wolves*. Paying attention and trusting that my life will yield necessary information to take forthcoming steps always pays off. When I first visited Pacifica to attend my friend's graduation, I got lost trying to find

the school. Driving through the hills of Santa Barbara became a purposeful and welcoming journey home. I knew that my academic path would lead me here.

I was raised in South Africa during apartheid. The masks my family wore to cover our internal familial pain were the same that afforded us a blind eye to our racial and class privilege that blatantly and violently oppressed the black people and other people of color in our homeland. My family, as with most other white families, adopted an attitude of complacency. With racial tensions rising, we left South Africa in 1986, not in protest of the atrocities against the black community, but rather to protect our privilege.

Did you make it through the first paragraph? It's tough to follow because the student was trying too hard to cover things she thought had to be laid out in the first paragraph. There's no flow. The second paragraph, however, is strong; each sentence connects to the next. When the student rewrote the essay, she completely deleted the first paragraph, and the rest evolved into a spectacular piece of writing.

Here's another example:

PROMPT

What's your favorite word and why?

> My favorite word is "sentient." Why? Well, first of all, it makes a good username . . .

This student commented himself that his opening "feels kind of generic." Yup. This is also an example of "giving away the goods" (discussed further in the next chapter). I reminded him that he did not have to respond directly to the prompt or address it right away. Here's the final version of the first paragraph:

> As an underclassman, I frequently experienced social anxiety. I also browsed the Internet regularly and, in some online circles, the word "robot" was used to refer to someone who lacked social and life skills. My anxiety tried to convince me that I was becoming a robot, but I wouldn't let that happen. I wanted change. I wanted to be confident, sociable, and proactive. So I adopted "sentient" as my username. In doing so, I was rejecting my fear that I was becoming "one of them." I had achieved sentience, if you will.

By waiting to reveal his word, the writer makes us curious. The entire essay (which is in the Appendix) has more impact because we learn a little about him first. That doesn't mean an essay couldn't successfully start with proclaiming your word, but this particular one worked better by waiting.

SLAP-ON ENDINGS

Opening sentences make first impressions, and closing sentences make lasting ones. I read essays that are sailing along, and then they slam into the rocks. Usually it's because the writer is plain old tired (not to mention sick and tired) of writing essays! So he throws something on the page because that's better than nothing. These slap-on endings are usually a series of statements or a recap. Zzzzzz. Not a great way to leave a lasting impression.

PROMPT

Describe an example of your leadership experience in which you have positively influenced others, helped resolve disputes, or contributed to group efforts over time.

. . . My experience volunteering at the summer camp has shaped me into who I am today. I have become more understanding and patient and have realized how impactful I can be.

Notice these sentences are statements (and off-prompt).

HERE'S THE REVISION—

. . . The fact that bullying was present in a camp environment upset me to the point where I decided to take action. I organized an assembly for all the campers, during which I talked about the different types of bullying so that the kids would become aware of how their derogatory comments can affect a person for the rest of their life. Over the following weeks, the kids became more kind to one another. They would give a hand if someone fell on the playground and even include Alex and Arianna in games. I felt gratified to see that my position as a leader not only positively impacted the kids, but also their environment.

When exhaustion is not the reason, a weak or nonending is often symptomatic of the need to get the preceding paragraph(s) in better shape. Once you do that, you should find a satisfactory ending. When possible, look for a way to wrap up your essay that applies what you have written to the "bigger picture" (there's a good example in the Appendix).

7

CONDENSING

WORD COUNT

Limits force you to write lean and clean. First drafts tend to go long by nature, so be aware of word count, but don't obsess too much about it early on. However, if there's a 250-word limit and you're running over a page, it's time to employ some "situational awareness," as my father the engineer would say.

Don't ever add sentences or words merely for the purpose of getting close to word count; likewise, don't fall too short. If it's a 650-word essay and you've only produced 350, that's insufficient. Either you haven't chosen a meaty enough topic or you haven't fully developed your response.

If you've made an editing pass and still exceed the word limit, try working in reverse. Print your essay so you can see the entire thing. Highlight "must keep" phrases and tighten the rest. Sometimes you can cut words here and there; other times, you have to go for entire phrases or sentences to make the count. It depends. If your dominoes will still fall without the word or phrase, cut it. This reverse tool is especially useful when you encounter a similar prompt with half the word count.

When all is said and done, what's more important than word count is making your words count.

KEEP IT SIMPLE, STUPID

I first learned about the KISS principle in an advertising class. The phrase is attributed to Kelly Johnson, who was a Lockheed Skunk Works engineer in the 1960s. Johnson felt that simplicity was a key goal in design and unnecessary complexity should be avoided. While I have impressed upon you repeatedly the importance of details in your writing, this is where I tell you that doesn't mean you include *every single detail* in your essays. As Alfred Hitchcock famously said,

What is drama but life with the dull bits cut out.

Classical dramatic structure has a beginning, middle, and end. The building blocks are scenes, and each scene also has a beginning, middle, and end, but you don't necessarily need to include all three in a scene (or play or movie) to make your point. As discussed earlier, playwrights and screenwriters are taught to enter a scene as late as possible and exit as early as possible. Sometimes a story starts in the middle or at the end, and the beginning may never be woven in because it is implied. These theories also apply to books (built upon chapters) and essays, which are constructed with paragraphs and sentences.

How much detail do you need? Only enough to get your points across. Lucky for you, the word count forces succinctness!

My involvement on campus led me to the University of California District of Columbia program. While in D.C., I was fortunate enough to land an incredible internship that further expanded my perception of the legal world. While interning for BET Networks in Washington D.C., I was able to focus on a new area of the law that was nothing less than electrifying: the world of entertainment law.

The student mentions the District of Columbia three times in one paragraph. And flowery language such as "incredible internship" and "nothing less than electrifying" needs to be replaced with language that tells us *why* the internship was incredible and *why* entertainment law seemed electrifying.

AFTER EDITING—
My involvement on campus led me to the University of California District of Columbia program. I interned at BET Networks, where I . . .

ANOTHER EXAMPLE—
One of the most disturbing factors of the film was the fact that the more McDonald's he ate, the more he craved it despite the damage it was doing to his body not only in gaining weight but in his cholesterol going up by sixty-five points.

The writer doesn't need to *tell* us about the damage being done to this person's body when she *shows* us:

What I found most disturbing was that the more "super-sized" meals he ate, the more he craved them, despite his weight and cholesterol levels increasing significantly.

Pithy writing keeps your reader engaged.

REDUNDANCIES

Repetitive words, phases, concepts, statements, and rhythm are the most common writing faux pas I see. They bog down a read, as well as highlight the wrong things. Early drafts are replete with this kind of overwriting; very rarely do you need to say something more than once. The easiest way to catch these flaws is to read your essay out loud, because repetitive words and phrases stick out like sore thumbs.

> She grabs herself a beer as I pour myself some iced tea before we head out to enjoy the summer evening in her garden. In the summer, we hang out in the backyard, watch the birds, and talk. I tease her about her orange, self-tanner-tinted skin. She claims she wants her hands and feet to be as pretty as Oprah's. I enjoy walking through her garden and harvesting squash, peppers, sunflowers, herbs, and tomatoes. We save some of the harvest for canning or for the dinner we will cook together later that evening . . .

Since it's warm enough to enjoy the evening in the garden, we don't need to be told it's summer, which also gets rid of the "summer" repeat. Likewise, we don't need to be told about the garden when the writer tells us about harvesting squash, etc. There's a word count, so minimizing irrelevant details and extraneous background information is crucial. Get to the point, because you must leave room for the substantive portion of your essay.

HERE'S THE REVISION—

> She grabs a beer from the frig and I pour myself some iced tea. Then we head out to enjoy the evening in her

garden. I harvest some squash, peppers, sunflowers, herbs, and tomatoes. We'll cook some up for dinner and save some for canning . . .

ANOTHER EXAMPLE—
Learning about the power of nutrition has influenced my career path. I feel compelled to spread this knowledge to others. As a dietician, I can help others heal from within by nourishing them with the power of what's on the plate.

This student doesn't need to mention the career path when she tells us that she wants to become a dietician. She also used "the power of what's on the plate" phrase in another essay for the same school, so she removed it here:

Learning about the power of nutrition has compelled me to spread the knowledge of healing from within to others as a dietician.

In the following first draft, the student writes about an influential person in her life. The essay has a strong concept and a memorable tag, but they get buried in an avalanche of repetitiveness and a run-on paragraph.

"Would you rather go through life on a merry-go-round or a roller coaster?" That's a frequent question that comes out of my mother's mouth. Over the years, my mom, who many of my friends refer to as "Lesson Mom," has shared many humorous and not-so-humorous teachable moments that stem from her own achievements, failures, and even embarrassments. As a result, I have learned that my mom wasn't born perfect; yet, more importantly, that she grew into the confident and capable person she is today from each one of these experiences. My mom's merry-go-round vs. roller coaster analogy is one of her "life lessons" that resonates with me most. Naturally being the adventure junky that I am, when she would ask me if I would prefer a merry-go-round or a roller coaster, my answer would always be a roller coaster. She, too, knew I would say a roller coaster. Given that roller coasters are comprised of ups, downs, curves, and spins, they provide for surprising and exciting experiences. However, on the other hand, merry-go-rounds are predictable and boring—they just go round and round and round. My mom then went on to tell me, life, too, is a roller coaster filled with highs, lows, curves, and spins. However, the important thing is to get back up on your feet when you are at a low or have been thrown a curve. She would further explain to me that this is how we grow, learn, and build character to take on the next hurdle in life. Then, she would claim that if life were an unadventurous and conventional merry-go-round, it would not provide for any personal growth. In other words, my mom was trying to say if you are knocked down off your feet, you have to find the strength, courage and knowledge to come back up—she'd always say consider it character building. To this day, I take my mom's (a.k.a. <u>Lesson Mom's</u>) inspiring words on <u>roller coasters</u> and other life experiences to heart. I have been greatly inspired by these stories, which have ultimately helped shape my outlook on life. More importantly, I am not afraid to take on challenge and, when I'm faced with an obstacle, I chuckle, pause, and then think of it simply as character building.

The lush forest lurking in this essay cannot be seen through the copious trees. Job one: Cut the redundancies. Job two: Omit the obvious (see next subchapter). Hopefully, you recognized that the writer devoted too much time to Lesson Mom; she also failed to tell us *how* she is an "adventure junky" and refers to the roller coasters of her life without giving an example. After the rewrite—

HERE'S THE REVISION—
"Would you rather go through life on a merry-go-round or a roller coaster?" That is a question that frequently comes out of my mother's mouth. Over the years, my mom, whom many of my friends refer to as "Lesson Mom," has shared many humorous and not-so-humorous teachable moments that stem from her own achievements, failures, and even embarrassments. Naturally, I was relieved to learn that my mom wasn't born perfect. Yet each of these, as she would

say, "character-building" experiences has helped shaped her into the confident and capable person she is today. And this inspires me.

My mom's merry-go-round vs. roller coaster analogy is her life lesson that resonates with me most. Being the adventure junky that I am (whether I am the first to take the plunge down a double black diamond while skiing or the most dangerous of waves while surfing), my answer has always been to take the surprise and excitement of the ups, downs, curves, and spins of a roller coaster over the predictable, repetitive, and boring movements of a merry–go-round. I have taken this analogy to heart, especially when confronted with situations when I've needed to be resilient and get back up on my feet. One such instance came into play in Middle School . . .

This writing is crisper, and the good content has been strengthened, which keeps the reader interested.

HINT

When rewriting, remember those dominoes. You cannot edit in a vacuum. Reread your entire essay whenever you make changes, as the new context may bring other issues to your attention.

DON'T TELL US THE OBVIOUS

In Chapter 3, I reminded you that readers come to essays dumb and blind, so you must clue them in with necessary details; now I'm telling you to remember that your readers aren't stupid! In other words, don't hit us over the head with that unnecessary close-up. Case in point: the "Lesson Mom" essay. We know that roller coaster rides are comprised of ups, downs, curves, and spins and merry-go-rounds go round and round. This student did not realize that she had us at hello. Her obvious descriptions were dead weight, but when she used those metaphors to describe her life, they transmuted into colorful prose.

Here's a subtler example from another student's opening paragraph:

As I board the plane, the flight attendant takes one look at my carry-on item and asks if I'm a dog trainer or a Hula Hooper. I smile, amused, as I explain that my hoop is one of the four apparatuses I use in rhythmic gymnastics.

Between "the flight attendant" and "carry-on," we know where the writer is, so she can lose the first phrase:

The flight attendant takes one look at my carry-on item and asks if I'm a dog trainer or a Hula Hooper. I smile, as I always do, and explain that my hoop is one of the four apparatuses I use in rhythmic gymnastics.

There is no need to tell us that she competes at either a national or international level, because the phrase "as I always do" implies that she travels quite a bit for her sport. This paragraph is also an excellent example of not hitting us over the head with your fabulousness (see next chapter).

Rambling like Jerry Maguire might be charming in a movie and can definitely be productive when brainstorming. But once you start editing, remove those overexplanations that take up too much precious word space and weigh down the reading experience.

DON'T GIVE AWAY THE GOODS

This common misstep, often made in first paragraphs, is when the writer telegraphs what he is going to tell us. This kind of writing blunts the impact of the points being conveyed.

PROMPT

What work of art, music, science, mathematics, or literature has surprised, unsettled, or challenged you, and in what way? (250 words)

When I was in the 9th grade, I read *Freakonomics* by Steven Levitt and Stephen Dubner. I was initially unsure if I'd like a book about economics but I had heard good things about it, both from other authors that I liked, and my teachers.

Before reading *Freakonomics*, I had thought that economics was a boring and stale topic. I thought that it was simply the study of markets and stocks and indexes, of meaningless abstract quantities that had no bearing on most people's lives. This book showed me that there was much more to economics. It was a way of explaining the way society works in a quantitative manner. I fell in love with the idiosyncratic way the book applied economic concepts to situations I never would have imagined had anything to do with economics . . .

Naming the book in the opening sentence makes for a dry start. There's no building drama.

HERE'S THE REVISION—
As a freshman, I thought that economics was a boring, stale topic—the study of markets and stocks and indexes, and meaningless abstract quantities that had no bearing on my life whatsoever. Then I read *Freakonomics* and fell in love with the idiosyncratic way the authors applied economic concepts to situations I never would have imagined—for example, how incentives can influence sumo wrestlers and teachers to act in similar ways . . .

By trimming the repetitive fat, moving things around, and providing detail, the writing becomes more interesting and engaging. Take a look at another student's first pass:

> Recently, I was able to communicate with a family at the museum in Vietnamese. During one of my shifts, I was holding a Smilodon skull to show visitors. While standing in the rotunda, I saw a Vietnamese family struggling to find their way in the museum. I proceeded to the family with the cat skull, and they were shocked with the object I was holding. I asked them if they needed help in Vietnamese.

This student does not need to tell us in the first sentence what is later revealed by her story.

HERE'S THE REVISION—
> During a recent shift, I was showing visitors a Smilodon skull when I saw a Vietnamese family struggling to find their way in the museum. I walked toward them, and they were shocked by the cat skull I was holding. Speaking Vietnamese, I asked if they needed help and they seemed relieved.

Telegraphing—or telling people what you'll tell them—is another form of repetition; remove it from your writing.

8

STYLE

Even if your writing has good content and emotion, poor style will become a distraction, like a beach ball being volleyed around a baseball stadium. This chapter discusses some of these distractions, as well as content that can repel readers.

SKIP THE BEAUTY PAGEANT STATEMENTS

You know what I'm talking about—declarations such as "I want to be a doctor because I want to help people" or "as an immigration attorney, I can give hope to those who are desperate for a safe haven."

Students tend to use these types of empty phrases because they don't know what else to say. Perhaps they think such proclamations make them appear to have purpose. Unfortunately, sappy statements stick with readers for the wrong reasons. Even if you sincerely do want to cure cancer or bring about world peace, you must find a way to say it so that readers don't picture you in a chiffon evening gown with a sash bearing the name of your home state or country.

The best way to sound sincere and passionate—but not trite—is to "show, don't tell" and get specific with descriptive details.

In virtual games, we can respawn, but on Earth, I will use big data to help my teammates around the world. I only have one life and I will make the most of it.

HERE'S THE REVISION—

Looking back, it seems that inspiration can arise from anything, anywhere—including a video game. Looking forward, whether I am creating prediction models for cancer or analyzing speech patterns for self-driving cars, I cannot wait to create lasting change as a big data scientist.

ANOTHER EXAMPLE—

On August 19, 2017, I attended my mom's citizen interview as her Spanish-speaking translator. While in the waiting room . . . Experiences like this have helped define the purpose I'd like for my life to have. Seeing the positive impact you can have on others by helping them navigate something foreign, however small it might be, has shaped me into who I am today and who I would like to be tomorrow. Since childhood my desire to help others has served as the catalyst in fueling my passion for law. For as long as I can remember I associated the law and lawyers as a means to help others when they feel the most helpless, so instinctively a career in law became my biggest aspiration. Today, I know that a career in law is the way that I will continue impacting other's lives in truly meaningful ways.

HERE'S THE REVISION—

Last August, I attended my mom's citizenship interview as her Spanish-speaking translator. While in the waiting room, I watched as an older Hispanic man was called up. I overheard that he would not be able to proceed because he did not bring a translator with him. Instinctively, I jumped up and offered my services. Having grown up in a migrant farm working community in California's Central Valley, I learned at a young age that speaking English was an asset, because I could be of assistance to my parents and the people around me. Translating documents for my parents or helping strangers communicate with a cashier at the store might not have seemed like much at the time, however these things laid the foundation for my desire to pursue a career in law.

EASY ON THE SCHMALTZ

Once your essay has burned off some sugar, it's time to cut the fat. Yiddish word of the day: *schmaltz*. The literal translation is "fat" or "grease," especially with regard to a chicken. The word also means "excessive sentimentality or mush." *Et voilà*, the Schmaltz-O-Meter. Avoid setting it off.

As with Beauty Pageant Statements, simply find another way to express what you are trying to say. Take a look at this excerpt from an essay about a significant educational opportunity:

> Working with my mentor has taught me the importance of being compassionate and relatable toward patients, because "good doctors treat the patient, not the disease." The more time I spent at Dr. B's office and the hospital, the more awestruck I became by the wonders and tragedies it held under the same roof. These moments motivate me to learn all that I can about medicine, so that one day, I might be able to save lives, just as Dr. B had saved mine.

This paragraph has several phrases that stack one on top of the other like pastrami on rye—it's oozing fat, not to mention there's a Beauty Pageant Statement!

Here's the final version, which has more detail and less empty calories:

> I continue to spend time learning from Dr. B and his team of medical professionals, and I also volunteer once a week at the information desk in the same teaching hospital. I give visitors directions and connect medical personnel with family members. The more time I spend at the hospital and Dr. B's office, the more awestruck I become by the wonders and tragedies occurring under one roof. Dr. B once told me "good doctors treat the patient, not the disease." Working with my mentor and his colleagues has encouraged me to become a lifelong learner and has solidified my desire to pursue a career in medicine.

Sometimes simple editing brings the Schmaltz-O-Meter rating into acceptable territory. For example, after deleting material and providing a change of context, the "good doctors treat the patient, not the disease" phrase becomes palatable.

In the following excerpt, the student, who explains he was using his big data skills to win computer games, started to rethink his pursuits when a friend became terminally ill:

. . . The light bulb in my head went off as the thought about how I could change the world by harnessing something greater than a computer game like millions, billions, even trillions of data points.

My work started off by extracting genomic DNA from blood leukocytes. With trillions of sequences in the human genome, I collected cancer-specific ones to train the algorithm, with my friend David in mind.

. . . I realized the war against cancer was something I couldn't do alone. It's a team effort, with thousands of people with different specialties around the world with one thing: data. With big data, I could use all the data to bridge the dichotomies around the world, to form my vision of a perfect universe—one without cancer.

This last paragraph not only could induce cavities but also strays from the prompt. The student forgot he was writing about his interest in big data and not the cure for cancer. What is working in this draft is that you can feel his passion; it's genuine. He just needed to harness his enthusiasm.

HERE'S THE REVISION—

. . . Then my friend David died from osteosarcoma at 18 years of age. My meaningless desires to farm green dragons and win LoL [*] games died with him.

---

* *League of Legends*

I thought, what if my world of big data could merge with David's dreams of a cure for cancer?

The easiest way to get rid of over-the-top language is to replace it with story:

It helped me to realize when you believe in others, you inspire them to believe in themselves.

HERE'S THE REVISION—
My most rewarding moments on the team have been when a teammate learns how far she has jumped and then runs up to me to celebrate a new personal record and thank me for having faith in her.

And while we're on the topic of schmaltz, avoid overusing the phrases "I fell in love with," "I love," and "I would love to"—whether you are referring to algebra or a school's campus. One of my students used the same "love" phrase in three of her four essays for the same school. When she read them out loud, she could hear how overblown they sounded. Also watch out for "I came to realize" and "I realized." Use these phrases sparingly, be sure the context is appropriate, and, most importantly, don't forget to tell us *why* you love something or *how* you came to realize something.

DON'T BRAG

Peppering your essay with particulars about your accomplishments and talents can get as tiresome as a blockbuster with stellar special effects but no story. There is a section in every application where you input your accomplishments and grades; let those sections do your bragging. If you start infusing essays with titles, awards, and achievements so admissions will know how awesome you are, that application will get dismissed. They'll wonder, did you do things out of genuine motivation and interest or just to build your resume? Bottom line: Statistics and name-dropping are a turn off.

PROMPT

Please briefly elaborate on one of your extracurricular activities or work experiences, using between 50–100 words.

In my third year serving in my high school's student government, I was elected vice president and school board representative. I am honored that my classmates had the confidence in me to help lead and represent the school. This experience has further cultivated my skills in organizing, communicating, interviewing, negotiating, presenting, motivating and leading others. Moreover, having the school district's superintendent approach me after my first school board presentation, commenting on my extraordinary poise and organization, was the icing on the cake. These real-life skills are invaluable and will serve me well in my future.

In addition to the statements and bragging, this essay would not survive the "can you pass your essay to the right?" test. After digging deeper into her experience making board presentations, the student wrote:

> As school vice president, I found myself presenting the status of campus events and programs to the district board. This crowd had a contentious reputation, and my speech was going to be streamed live. With my talking points before me, I decided to improvise. When I humorously said, "In my senior year, I finally have a class—financial algebra—that will be useful in life," I got laughs. I had connected and felt my confidence building. Student government has given me my favorite moments in school, from attending board meetings to pumping up fans while dressed as Marvin the Mustang.

If any of your essay sounds like a list, you are likely bragging. Instead, look for the story within the accomplishment—a particular experience or someone you met—and *that's* what you write about. Your accomplishments and qualities will *subtly* come across. You can mention titles and accomplishments, if they're necessary or relevant, but present them within the context of your story.

> As a sophomore, I did some part-time consulting for Disney in Shanghai.

By giving this gig context and going beyond the name-drop, the paragraph steps back from the brag:

> I put what I was learning into practice at a consulting project at Disney Shanghai. My job was to research and prepare reports on changing consumer demographics with regard to the development of the Star Wars franchise in China.

I recall one student who, like so many others, set out to write about his summer volunteering in a remote and poor village on another continent. I had recently heard an interview on NPR's *This American Life* where the director of undergraduate admissions at Georgia Institute of Technology was asked what essays he and his colleagues were sick of reading. He sighed in such a way that I could almost see his eyes roll across the airwaves: "The mission trip essay!" Then he said, ". . . When you first start reading that essay, you're like, 'Oh, here it comes again!'" Trying to convince my student to steer clear of the "I set out to change their lives, but they ended up changing mine" cliché, I asked him, "Did you meet anyone memorable on this trip?" "Yeah," he said without hesitating, "the elderly Japanese man sitting next to me on the plane." At first, this student was not too thrilled about his seat partner, but he ended up talking to him for hours. *This* is what the student wrote about. Incidentally, the student was able to slip into the essay that he was on his way to volunteer in a foreign country, but the crux of the writing was the older man's profound effect on him.

Did you notice in the previous examples how telling the story makes the writers unique? They are no longer just another student council vice president, a statistics whiz interning at a high-tech company, or a volunteer on a summer mission. They are now distinct and memorable applicants.

AVOID BROWNNOSING

By the same token, when writing those application "why" essays, no kissing the colleges' you-know-what! They already know their school and alumni network are great, and they don't need you to tell them. This kind of sap will not score you points. Your fix for this red flag is to replace the statements with relevant detail.

> . . . I aspire to begin my journey as a big data scientist at NYU and spend the upcoming years <u>at the leading university of computer science and culture</u>.

HERE'S THE REVISION—
. . . In this way, merging Big Data and Economics feels natural to me, especially in regard to public

health policy. I'd like to study how economic incentives could be utilized to combat America's obesity epidemic. NYU's Computer Science and Economics joint major will assist me in this empirical approach to Economics.

WATCH YOUR TONE

I may sound like your mother, but if you sound like an angry, bitter, snotty, arrogant, or spoiled teenager, your application will get grounded. Maybe you are angry about something, or maybe you have been spoiled. If this is what you want to write about, be sure to show some progression or insight on your part. *How* you express yourself and come across is what counts. And then there is that raw teenage emotion that can surface in brainstorming and first drafts:

> I don't feel judged by my peers; however, I feel as if my parents are constantly judging me. My peers have accepted me and I don't care what most of them think anyways. My parents judge my social and academic choices, my eating and sleeping habits, etc., as most parents should. Sometimes they think I spend too much time with my boyfriend when I could be studying . . .

While this paragraph has many issues—failure to relate specifics to the reader (e.g., *what* are the choices she is making? And *who* is "them"?), an unnecessary stilted transition, and word repetition—let's focus on the tone. Having the strength to not care what others think about you is a good thing, but this student does not come off as likeable. Maybe you're thinking this student *is* snotty, so the tone is genuine. Fact is, I knew this student, and how she presented on paper was not in line with her real demeanor. By filtering her unfettered emotions and providing context for her point, she was able to change everything:

> Since most of my friends live near our school in the Palisades thirty minutes away, my sister left for college two years ago, and my dad has been travelling for numerous business trips, I feel lonely at times. Krissy has always been there for me. At her home, I forget about all the stress, whether it's schoolwork, a fight with my mom, or getting tired of hearing my parents tell me I spend too much time socializing or with my boyfriend when I should be studying. I understand they are my parents, so they should be on top of my grades and how I spend my time, but Krissy isn't my mom. She doesn't have to care how much time I spend with any one person or if I'm getting that A in calculus . . .

WRITE INSIDE

Have you ever noticed that many new parents talk to their babies and toddlers in third person? "Mommy loves you!"

"Daddy is upset you threw your peas on the floor!" When children start talking, however, they don't talk this way! Think about what the child is actually hearing: a parent who is removed from the conversation or request, at a distance. I often see students keep this same distance from their application essays even when they are writing in first person. I call this "writing outside."

Sometimes a word change here and there does the trick. Let's examine several examples where shifts in person and voice made all the difference.

This student, who was applying to a music program. not only changed the point of view but also added more detail.

OUTSIDE—

I can feel the energy of the music and see it in the faces of the audience all the way to the students in the last row.

INSIDE—

The waves of energy sent out by the tense phrases of this quaint Russian folk tune gone wild travel through the Shed all the way to my student seat in the last row.

Here's another writer who was able to move from an almost clinical perspective to a more personal and powerful paragraph.

OUTSIDE—

Only with the expertise of a neurologist was my family able to find some stability amidst the chaos. He explained the transient ischemia in the brain had caused significant necrosis and presented concrete evidence to back up his determination of brain death.

INSIDE—

It wasn't until we talked to the neurologist that my family and I were able to find some stability amidst the chaos. With patience and sensitivity, Dr. Jones guided us through the CT scans and neurological test, and he presented concrete evidence to back up his determination that my father was brain dead.

Can you locate and identify the shifts in these examples?

OUTSIDE—

In this way school was like running—if you wanted to succeed, you'd have to push yourself to do better. You wouldn't make the cut for competitive meets by taking it easy in practice. How did I expect myself to do well if all I did was play video games instead of do homework?

INSIDE—

School, then, was like running—I didn't quality for competitions by taking it easy in practice, so how did

I expect myself to do well in school if all I did was play Ancient Domains of Mystery on my laptop during class?

OUTSIDE—

TCU* dietetic students recently teamed up with medical students from UNTHSC* to bridge the gap between nutrition and medicine through a Culinary Medicine course. Through this partnership, TCU students get a look at what they will be practicing after they graduate as well as showing that eating healthy doesn't have to be boring.

INSIDE—

As I want to use food to heal rather than medications, I am also interested in the recent partnership of TCU dietetic students with medical students from UNTHSC in the Culinary Medicine course.

That last first draft reads like a description from the TCU course catalog. And that's never good. Application essays are *personal* essays. Make sure your writing doesn't sound like an encyclopedia entry, academic paper, or subject essay for English class. Own it. Make it yours.

[Write inside.]

*Texas Christian University and the University of North Texas Heath Science Center

9

POLISHING

LOSE OR REPLACE STILTED TRANSITIONS

An essay loaded with transitions such as "in addition," "furthermore," "therefore," and "finally" is usually a result of flow deficiency. First of all, these devices make your writing sound formulaic and boring. Therefore, all those transitional words and other writing devices you learned in English comp, for example "for example"—fuggedaboutem! In addition, overuse of these transitions makes your essay sound as though you weren't quite sure how to move from one point to the next, so you threw one in as a link.

If such transitions turn up repeatedly in your writing,

view them as red flags marking writing weaknesses or flow problems. Furthermore, keep in mind that good writing almost always replaces the need for these transitions. And finally, since these words and phrases tend to screech like fingernails on a chalkboard, reducing their presence makes the ones you purposefully choose less intrusive.

Here's the first paragraph of this section without all those stilted transitions:

> An essay loaded with transitions, such as "in addition," "furthermore," "therefore," and "finally," is usually a result of flow deficiency. These devices make your writing sound formulaic and boring, so all those transitional words and other writing devices you learned in English comp—fuggedaboutem! Overuse of these transitions makes your essay sound as though you weren't quite sure how to move from one point to the next, so you threw one in as a link.

CAN YOU TASTE YOUR ESSAY?

Chef Emeril Lagasse favors spicier cuisines, such as Creole and Cajun. Pretend that he is going to eat your essay. Will he find intense flavor? Will it melt in his mouth and make him want more? Will he want to share the dish with his colleagues? Or will he send your bland writing back to the kitchen and tell you to "kick it up a notch!"? The ingredients of your essay should deliciously combine to make your readers in admissions want to savor it. As that last word lingers on their tongues, you want them to shout, "BAM!"

> It's not just what you write but how you write it.

Are you using the juiciest verbs possible?

> I usually run to her house. Maybe it's because I'm excited or maybe it's because I'm a runner and it's just a quicker way to get around . . . I <u>head</u> across my neighbor's lawn . . . and <u>pass</u> a few more homes . . .

This writer was anxious to get to her destination, and this edited version reflects that with more robust verbs:

> I usually run to her house. Maybe it's because I'm excited or maybe it's because I'm a runner and it's just a quicker way to get around. I <u>cut</u> across my neighbor's lawn, and <u>dash</u> past a few more homes . . .

ANOTHER EXAMPLE—

I began to wonder if my own junk food would affect my athletic performance, and I took into account <u>how I felt after</u> a greasy hamburger or scrambled eggs with bacon.

BECOMES—

The more I learned about nutrition, the more I saw the correlation between <u>how I felt after chowing down</u> chocolate chip pancakes with bacon versus a Greek salad with tahini dressing.

The change to "chowing down" makes more impact. The student also strengthened a run-of-the-mill "greasy hamburger" to one of her other junk food favorites, "chocolate chip pancakes with bacon."

ANOTHER EXAMPLE—

They would <u>talk</u> to each other regarding what I had confided . . .

BECOMES—

They would <u>gossip</u> to other classmates about what I had confided . . .

You can also spike your adjectives, but don't cross that line into flowery language. Juicy verbs and adjectives serve a purpose; they aren't just frivolous adornment. And while you're checking that the words in your essay are as piquant as possible, look for any lingering phrases that could use some spicing up.

> Sometimes, I need a little creaminess but I cannot
> find something buttery, so I substitute in coconut sor-
> bet instead.

The detail about sorbet was good, but I asked this student to get more specific about the time she needed to use it:

> Once, when there was nothing buttery left in the pan-
> try for an Alfredo sauce, I substituted coconut sorbet.
> A little strange for my palate, but it worked.

> **If you have established a simile or**
> **metaphor, are you relishing it?**

Sometimes these devices are best left at one sentence, but if you come up with one, look for ways to spin it. Like a comedian on a roll with a gag, work the room. Just don't overdo it. Once again, the best way to catch "too much" is to read your essay out loud to someone. They will tell you where it is and isn't working, and you'll likely hear it too. (I use an extended metaphor in this section, and there's another example in the Appendix.)

THE "IT" WORD

Charles Dickens may have opened his classic novel *A Tale of Two Cities* with "It was the best of times, it was the worst of times," but *most* of the time, sentences are crisper and better when they don't start with "it."

It wasn't easy in the beginning; each move seemed like the most difficult situation I had ever been in.

BECOMES—

In the beginning, each move seemed like the most difficult situation I had ever been in.

The freshmen disrespected both our coach and the other players. They would consistently not warm up at matches, and their performance in match play was then affected. It would be common to see them go up 4–1, only to end up losing.

BECOMES—

The freshmen disrespected our coach as well as other players. They would consistently not warm up before matches, and their play was then affected. They would commonly run up a 4–1 lead, only to end up losing.

It was from this experience that I began to consider becoming a sports therapist.

BECOMES—
This experience made me consider becoming a sports therapist.

_____

It is important to me to have a place where I feel completely safe expressing my thoughts and opinions

BECOMES—
Having a place where I feel completely safe expressing my thoughts and opinions is important to me.

THE "THERE" WORD

The same theory applies to starting sentences with "there."

There is something about the serenity and quiet atmosphere that makes me really enjoy golf.

BECOMES—
The serenity and quiet atmosphere are what I enjoy most about golf.

_____

There was nothing more gratifying than to see that I not only positively impacted someone, but an environment.

BECOMES—

I felt gratified to see that I not only positively impacted the kids but also their environment.

GOT RHYTHM?

Do too many sentences start the same way? Are all the sentences in one paragraph the same length? Do you run out of oxygen before you have finished a particular sentence? Does a paragraph read like a list? Alliteration and parallel construction are effective when they are deliberate and working, but all else is a sign of an unfinished piece of writing. Read your essay out loud to catch rhythm repeats and glitches. Then, have someone read it to you.

I remember the first time I visited New York. I was fourteen years old and went to see my eldest sister at NYU. I remember eagerly leaning out of her 10th floor dorm window, I was captivated . . .

Both sentences start the same way. The rewrite addressed the repetitive words, as well as replaced the similar "visited" and "went to see," and "New York" and "NYU":

I was fourteen years old when I first visited my eldest sister at NYU. Eagerly leaning out of her 10th floor dorm window, I was captivated . . .

Rhythm and tempo can also be useful tools to set a mood or feeling. If you're talking about something tense or fast paced, employ short sentences with a staccato feel, not long, lingering ones. (A good example of using tempo to heighten the drama is the opening paragraph of the math essay in the "Watch Your Language" subchapter.)

GUIDANCE FOR INTERNATIONAL STUDENTS

As mentioned previously, one pitfall for students applying in their second language is misinterpreting a prompt. Another is committing a language faux pas.

> Stingo, you look . . . you look very nice;
> you're wearing your cocksucker.

Meryl Streep, playing a Polish immigrant to Brooklyn, delivered this line in the one moment of levity in the otherwise intense film *Sophie's Choice*. The word her character was looking for was "seersucker," a type of fabric. Accidents happen, especially in a second language. Whether you are a Chinese student applying to an American school or an American student applying to a French school, this dialogue is a great example of why a native speaker should review your essay before you submit it. He can look for blatant blunders as well as places where your words don't reflect your intent.

Languages are complex, full of many nuances and

figures of speech. I am not advising that a native speaker should completely polish your essay so that its grammar and syntax are flawless; I find that a few spots where your writing isn't perfect can make it genuine.

I remember attending a press conference at a sporting event where an athlete who was still fine-tuning her command of the English language said, "I was a wastebasket out there today." Everyone who heard her knew she meant "basket case," but this mistake was endearing, not embarrassing.

If I ran across Streep's lines in a student's essay, I would recommend deleting or correcting the seersucker gaffe, but I would leave the athlete's wastebasket substitution. No harm, no foul with the latter; just a smile. And there is no confusion as to meaning.

Complete language purification would also diminish or change your essay's voice. What if the school calls to interview you and discovers your speaking skills are not consistent with your writing skills? They would naturally question whether you'd written the essay. Therefore, have your native reader concentrate on clarifying areas where your essay is confusing, disjointed, or misleading but not eliminating charming—and memorable—shortcomings.

READ YOUR DRAFT OUT LOUD

I cannot stress enough the importance of this exercise! Often, and especially when you think you are finished, step away from the computer! Print your essay, and with a pencil in hand, read it out loud. For some reason, we see things on paper that we do not see on a computer screen, and we hear things that don't necessarily register on paper. Listen for and identify the things we have discussed:

- Circle redundant words, phrases, and concepts
- Note where rhythm is rocky or repetitive
- Mark where you stumble or run out of breath
- Circle stilted transitions
- Write an *F* where one sentence doesn't flow to the next or you abruptly switch gears
- Write a *?* if something doesn't make sense
- Circle verbs that change tense or could use some beefing up
- Write a *V* if you have switched point of view or voice
- Draw horizontal lines separating each prompt point discussion to gauge whether you've properly balanced your attention (not too much here and not enough there)

When you feel you have exhausted this technique, have someone else read to you while you follow along, copy in hand. Anywhere they stumble or hesitate, take note. These "bumps" can provide tremendous insight because this person is new to the material (possibly, even, to the subject matter). Someone with fresh eyes and ears may also raise issues you hadn't thought of or interpret something you've written in a way you never intended.

After my students have cut their teeth on an essay or two, they begin to develop an "ear" for their writing. Whether they are reading out loud or I am, my students start to *hear* essay problems before I can even comment. A well-crafted essay will seamlessly trip from start to finish like a snake made of dominoes, so keep editing until you find the overall design that works.

ASSEMBLING THE ENTIRE PACKAGE

I had a student who began all four of her UC essays with a quote. She didn't notice this while working on the essays individually, but later, when she read them all together. These similar openings were distracting and made her writing seem formulaic.

Review your *entire* essay package for one school as a whole, which includes reading your essays out loud and in succession. Are there any sore thumbs sticking out, such as repeating phrases or words? Is there a healthy mix, or are all of your essays humorous or too serious? Consider the flow and tone of your complete package in the same way you evaluated each individual essay. Also be sure that each essay touches on a different aspect of you or your life.

10

PUT YOUR ESSAY TO THE TEST

With your essay on paper (and the prompt and word count at the top!), run though the following checklist:

1 Does your essay make an inviting visual impression (i.e., are there enough paragraph breaks)?

2 Are you within word or character count?

3 Are you dangerously below the required word count?

4 Have you addressed all points in the prompt?

5 Have you given these points the appropriate weight and attention they deserve?

6 Does the opening sentence or paragraph engage your reader?

7 Have you buried your lede?

8 Have you strayed off topic?

9 Have you fixated on your essay's subject matter (whether topic or person) to the point where you've disappeared?

10 Are you bragging anywhere?

11 Are you brownnosing anywhere?

12 Have you checked your tone?

13 Have you told us the obvious anywhere?

14 Has all unnecessary telegraphing been edited?

15 If you've used a quote, does it feel natural and appropriate in your essay's context?

16 Have you removed or replaced redundant words and phrases?

17 Did you delete or condense repetitive concepts?

18 Have you removed and replaced stilted transitions with stronger writing?

19 Did you rework sentences starting with "it" or "there"?

20 Are tenses and point of view consistent? If you meant to break the rules, does it work?

21 Have you replaced all statements with substance, stories, and details?

22 Have you toned down, removed, or replaced all Beauty Pageant Statements?

23 Is the Schmaltz-O-Meter going off anywhere?

24 Are you writing inside?

25 Have you used strong verbs and adjectives without overwriting?

26 Can a layperson still follow your essay, even if it contains necessary jargon?

27 If you are writing in a second language, has a native speaker reviewed your essay?

28 Have you printed your essay and read it out loud (several times!)?

29 Does your essay have good rhythm, with a variety of sentence starts and structures, from start to finish?

30 Has someone else read your essay to you one last time?

31 Could any other student turn in your essay?

32 Has your essay stopped talking to you?

If you can answer yes to that last question, congratulations! Your essay is finished!

BUT WAIT!

You must now consider whether your *entire package* for one school works well as a whole:

1 Does each essay in the package have a unique topic or angle?

2 Are different tones evident in your essays?

3 Have you applied the Domino Theory of Editing to the entire package?

4 If the answer is yes, read everything out loud one more time. Then, have someone read the entire package to you.

If all systems are go, submit!

11

PARTING ADVICE

DON'T PROCRASTINATE

Start working months ahead of your first deadline. This way, you'll have the necessary time amid all of your other activities and responsibilities to write quality essays. If you are working with a writing coach, teacher, or counselor, keep in mind that as deadlines approach, that adviser will not be as readily available or as keenly focused, thanks to students who've waited until the last minute to seek help! My most successful students have been those who planned and wrote early.

PUBLIC OR PRIVATE SCHOOL?

If you cannot obtain a scholarship to cover or significantly help with private school tuition, be sure to ask yourself and your parents if the expense (or debt!) is affordable and worth it. I have attended both public and private institutions and received an excellent education at all of them. And they all have strong alumni networks. There is also plenty of research out there that supports the notion that attending a private school may not be worth the investment.

APPLY FOR SCHOLARSHIPS

Speaking of tuition, there is a lot of money out there for scholarships (not to be confused with financial aid, which must be paid back!), but that is the subject of another book. Some excellent sources are listed here:

Cappex	www.cappex.com
Chegg	www.chegg.com
College Board	www.collegeboard.org
CollegeNET	www.collegenet.com
Fastweb	www.fastweb.com
Peterson's	www.petersons.com
Scholarships.com	www.scholarships.com
Unigo	www.unigo.com

WARNING

Scholarship applications require you to write
more essays! The good news: You can likely draw
content from your college application essays!

WORK THE INTERVIEW

If a school requires or requests an interview, prepare. Interviews can take place during a visit to campus or be arranged with alumni who live near you. Prior to your interview, make a list of some of your own questions about the school and your program or major. Bring these notes with you, and take notes during your interview, because you might receive information you want to remember. You might also come up with a new question during your conversation.

Need an icebreaker? Ask why alumni chose the school or what their favorite memories are.

If this is the first time you have been interviewed, practice. Have someone play the interviewer, record the conversation, and review the video. Be aware of how you are sitting and holding your hands. If you are in a chair that swivels, ground your feet. If you are high-strung or nervous, exercise or go for a brisk walk beforehand. Dress and groom appropriately. Even if your interview takes places over the phone or Internet, dress accordingly.

Breathe. Smile (naturally, of course). Listen to what the other person is saying and then respond. If you go in with just your agenda or expect your interviewer to do all the work, conversation will not come easily, and you will feel as if you are on a bad date. And so will the alumni.

CHECK YOUR EGO

You may have been flying banners for your dream school or your parents' alma mater since you were a kid. But that school may not offer your major, it might not accept you, or the tuition may not be affordable. Going to another school is not the end of the world. There are countless good institutions of higher learning in and beyond the United States, so check your ego at the ivy wall when selecting schools. See what comes up as you explore your options. Focus on the schools that accept you, and forget about the ones that don't. The application process can be fickle, so don't try to figure it out; just go with it.

Once you receive your acceptances, make your final choice for the right reasons. One of my students received early admission to three stellar universities, including two in the Ivy League, but she was wait-listed by a third Ivy League school. She was determined to get into that school as well and started an appeal letter, which was basically another "why" essay. Three drafts later, I still felt the essay was falling flat. "Do you really want to go to this school?" I asked the student. "Or are you determined to get accepted so you can say you got in, and then you're going to go to [X], because that's where you really want to go?" The next day, this student told me she was dropping her appeal.

BE TRUE TO YOUR SCHOOL AND YOURSELF

As a writing coach, my goal is for my students to become better writers in general. You will be writing a lot in school and, regardless of your later profession, business. We live in the Information Age, so hone those communications skills! And most importantly, relish your college experience—in the classroom, on campus, and in the community. The years go swiftly, but the memories, friends, and knowledge last a lifetime.

APPENDIX

A few more of my favorite essays follow. Don't just read them; study them. Break down the prompts, and analyze how the essays have been constructed. Think about how they move you, why they leave an impression, and what you learn about the students who wrote them. Also be aware of the writer's craft (a result of many passes!), the details that catch your attention, and the crisp writing that sticks to the prompt.

Pulling off humor is not easy, and the following essay does a great job doing it. The last paragraph is also a good example of finding the "bigger picture" when wrapping up an essay.

--- **PROMPT** ---

Recount an incident or time when you experienced failure. How did it affect you, and what lessons did you learn? (650 words)

We dubbed it "The Chicken." A skeleton of clear, Sharpie-stained plastic, dangling metal supports, and wiggling screws and gears draped in thin, artsy webs of glue-string. It looked as if my partner Edward and I had spent, at most, four or five hours on this forlorn creature, but in truth, we had devoted at least forty hours of planning, sawing, building, dismantling, and building again. The result: an inadequate robot arm that could not even remain upright without the helpful nudge of Edward's fingers.

As we stood in line to showcase our skills, there I was, clutching the wobbling mess and dreading my impending humiliation. Why, oh why, out of all the subjects in Science Olympiad, did I choose Robot Arm? I braced myself as we shuffled out to the floor. The timer beeped, and we began. The Chicken jerked and whirred, flopped to the right, dragged its useless claw sweepingly across its range—managing to knock a few pencils into the goal zone—then swung around to slash my arm, where I now proudly bear a scar. In a last ditch effort to impress its audience, the arm reared up and fell backwards, lacking the power to pull itself upright, then twitched erratically, never to move again. Edward and I settled back on our heels, resigned and relieved, barely suppressing giggles. The crowd was in hysterics, and my classmates pointed and chortled. Even the judges were stealthily lifting their lab goggles to wipe away tears of laughter. It was embarrassing, yet strangely delightful, to behold this spell of hilarity.

As I shakily gathered The Chicken in my arms and stumbled off the floor, I realized that the experience had not been so horrible after all. In fact, it was invigorating and refreshing. In the midst of a tense and nerve-wracking event, we had brought some relaxation and laughter with our ridiculous failure. I had walked into that room fully expecting disappointment and shame. Instead, by accepting the fact that there was nothing I could do, I devoted myself to making the most of what I had in the moment: a dysfunctional robot and, more importantly, my own attitude. By doing so, I unexpectedly experienced the highest point of my day.

With a positive outlook, I can turn any experience into a success, although not necessarily in the way that I had originally expected. This mindset proved especially valuable when I conducted stem cell research at The Scripps Research Institute last summer. During the interview, my mentor asked me, "How well are you able to handle disappointment? You know, research isn't like anything else—things will not work out more often than they will, and it's important that you don't get discouraged." Her words proved true; my assays were unsuccessful or inefficient on the first, second, and third tries—the percentages from the flow cytometer were too low, and my cells somehow died over the weekend. However, each "failure" was an opportunity for me to gain a deeper understanding and pester my mentor with questions. The process of finally landing on the right assay ultimately taught me more than the final solution.

I used to be cautious with my art, as well. Obsessed with perfection and used to winning every competition I entered, I was unwilling to take chances with new techniques. Now I've delved into other mediums and pushed my boundaries. I've learned to discover what I'm capable of, regardless of what the outcome might be.

Bringing this attitude forward with me into life, especially considering my chosen career in science, is crucial. "Failure" or unexpected outcomes have resulted in many revolutionary discoveries, such as penicillin and x-rays. By letting go of my pride and fear of inadequacy, I can enjoy an experience for what it is. I'm proud to have gotten something valuable out of that Science Olympiad competition: a new mentality of steadfast optimism that can prop open windows of possibility.

The following essays show how two people writing about the same thing can tell two completely different stories. The opening paragraph of the first essay also successfully employs an extended metaphor.

PROMPT

Every person has a creative side, and it can be expressed in many ways: problem solving, original and innovative thinking, and artistically, to name a few. Describe how you express your creative side. (350 words)

When I am in my kitchen, I create an intricate dance between different ingredients. Whether I'm transforming butter and shallots into an elegant waltz-like cream base under scallops or turning jalapeños, tomatoes, and onions into a tango-like fire in a mango salsa, I transform the ingredients, the same way a choreographer transforms her dancers.

Cooking is not just an art to me; it is about finding that mouthwatering intersection of interactions between chemicals and creativity. The formulation of each dish is a puzzle of the very best kind, because there is no one correct answer. Once, when making an Alfredo sauce, I could not find anything buttery in the pantry, so I substituted coconut sorbet instead. A little strange for my palate, but it worked. As long as I am open to my imagination, there is always something I can try, which has been good to learn for outside of the kitchen.

Each dish I build has numerous moving parts, so sometimes things don't go to plan. Whether it is learning that acid curdles milk when adding lemon juice to milk tea or burning pot stickers because I didn't put enough oil in the pan, I am constantly adapting. However, no matter what goes wrong, my kitchen is still my happy place where I am not limited by the rules and conventions that I face at school or at home. When I take out my mixing bowl and cutlery, the minutes that usually whiz by suddenly seem like hours and the stress of exams melts away. The cool marble countertop, the shiny stainless steel appliances, the nicked chopping board . . . the kitchen is my sanctuary, where I am free to create and explore.

PROMPT

Tell us about a personal quality, talent, accomplishment, contribution, or experience that is important to you. What about this quality or accomplishment makes you proud and how does it relate to the person you are? (1000 words total between this and another essay)

Fifty sticks of butter, ten cups of white sugar, twelve cups of brown sugar, sixteen cups of chocolate chips . . . sounds more like a recipe for diabetes than for my biggest and proudest accomplishment yet. Never in my life did I, a sixteen-year-old high schooler with no professional baking experience, imagine that I could cater desserts for a 200-guest wedding from my own kitchen.

This opportunity came about when my cousin got engaged and asked me to cater the deserts for her wedding. We had gathered in the kitchen to bake many times before, and there we were again: brainstorming ideas, scouring the Internet for recipes, and doing test runs. Not everything about the assignment was something that I naturally enjoy doing. I love the hands-on part of baking, but I still had to list and number crunch ingredients on spreadsheets, create budgets, and calculate timetables, often late into the night. I surprised even myself with the amount of organization and planning I did. After weeks of grueling prep work, I stood before my mother's double ovens, equipped with my trusted spatula, prepared to take on the army load of ingredients stacked on the counter.

Baking is a crapshoot—you never really know if your creation is going to turn out all right. You can't taste as you go like chefs do in cooking; it's chemistry, so there's always a chance of things going wrong in the oven. The sheer size of this project was a bit daunting, however, the next day after assembling hundreds of mini apple pies with the sweatshop crew my cousin sent over to help me that morning, I anxiously peered through the window of the oven door. As the minutes ticked by and the scent of caramelized sugar and melted butter began to pervade the house, the dough puffed into the perfect apple pie crust. I sighed in relief and turned my attention to the next batch.

When I saw all those mini apple pies, cookies, panna cotta, and cream puffs spread out across an elegant white table, I felt extremely proud. The wedding guests reminded me of patrons in an art gallery—except that my creations could be enjoyed not only with the eyes, but also with the palate.

The feeling of being stretched beyond my perceived limits is what drives me to take on challenges, even during my time of leisure. Being able to surpass my own expectations is like finding chocolate chips in an oatmeal cookie—a pleasant delight.

The next three essays were written by the same student and are a good example of borrowing content from one essay to use in another. In this case, the student adapted content from her Common App essay into two of her University of California essays.

──────── **PROMPT** ────────

Some students have a background, identity, interest, or talent that is so meaningful they believe their application would be incomplete without it. If this sounds like you, then please share your story. (650 words)
──────────

I used to feed myself junk nearly every day by scooping each lettuce leaf in ranch dressing and then drowning my ice cream with caramel sauce. I never understood what cholesterol was or the difference between vitamins and nutrients. I simply did not care what I was eating or how it was affecting me until I joined my high school's track team. A nutritionist came to talk to the athletes, and she showed us *Super Size Me*. In this documentary, the filmmaker tests the repercussions of a "McDonald's only" diet on himself. I found it most disturbing that the more "super-sized" meals he ate, the more he craved them, despite his weight and cholesterol levels increasing significantly.

I started to watch more food documentaries. *Hungry for Change* made me think about eating foods for a purpose rather than mindlessly; *GMO OMG* educated me about the history of genetically modified organisms and their possible repercussions on future generations. Then I watched *Cowspiracy* and learned that in California alone, we each use about 1,500 gallons of water a day, half of which is from the production of meat and dairy products.

The more I learned, the more I became aware of how I felt after chowing down on a greasy hamburger or chocolate chip pancakes with bacon. I wondered if my diet was affecting my athletic performance and causing my mood swings. Wanting to take back my health, I started to look up recipes for anything from green smoothies to stir frys to veggie burgers. I came across Tess Begg, an online vegan food blogger whose meals were bountiful and enticing. She attributed being able to keep up with her intense workouts to the abundance of plant foods in her diet. As a long and triple jumper, I noticed I was burning out physically during training in the off-season. Watching Tess's videos, I began to understand the repercussions of my negative relationship with food and learned ways to recover by changing what was on my plate.

I continued my research for eight months before I consciously decided not to eat meat. My transition was anything but easy. My parents assumed I wasn't getting enough iron, calcium and other nutrients. To address their concerns, I logged my food into

Chronometer.com to track my daily food intake. I was well beyond the targeted values for everything, except vitamin B12 because it is not naturally found in plant foods, so I started to take a supplement. Having proof that my new diet was sufficient, my parents believed I was being responsible and allowed me to continue.

Though it's hard to get through the after-football-game tradition of going to In-N-Out, I decided to look at veganism not as a restriction, but as a way to expand how I viewed food. From tofu pad Thais to Indian curries, I was tasting cuisine from different cultures and complex flavors. As a vegan, I could explore food options without harming the environment, make choices that align with my ethics, and feel more energized.

My older brother came over one day and asked me to make him an Instagram-worthy smoothie bowl as a joke. But when friends started saying "Make me one!," I began to plate other dishes in an aesthetic manner, then experimented with food photography. Ever since, I've published my meals to my Instagram page, @foodbyjan, to motivate others to rethink their eating habits. Now, my friends and family are excited to see what I bring to gatherings and share my profile with others.

Veganism has offered a way for me to go beyond my comfort zone and be my own person. It has also given me a way to explore my creativity, as well as influenced me to pursue a career in nutrition. As a registered dietician, I plan to use food to help heal people back to health.

PROMPT

Every person has a creative side, and it can be expressed in many ways: problem solving, original and innovative thinking, and artistically, to name a few. Describe how you express your creative side. (350 words)

"How does this look?" I ask my mother before I snap the photo. Of course, she always says it's fine, but being a perfectionist, I wonder if there is anything more I could do to make my plate look more appetizing. Should I swirl my berry smoothie? Fan an avocado over the Mexican-themed salad? Drizzle peanut sauce on a Buddha bowl? The possibilities always seem endless.

I began my journey with food photography when my older brother came over one day and asked me to make him an Instagram-worthy smoothie bowl as a joke. But when friends started saying, "I want one!," I began to plate all my dishes in an aesthetic manner and continued to experiment with food styling. Ever since, I've published my creations to my Instagram page, @foodbyjan, to motivate others to rethink their eating habits. Now, my friends and family are excited to see what I have whipped up and share my account with others.

Each day I challenge myself to think of new nutritious meals and how to make them look delicious to the largest audience possible. For some, it's balancing the colors of the vibrant fruits and vegetables; for others, it's about layering the different ingredients evenly or taking the photos from multiple perspectives to find the best angle.

Just like painting or writing can be an outlet for some, "food art" has become my stress reliever. Not only have I become my own person through my culinary designs, but I have gone beyond my comfort zone. Experimenting with food has given me a way to explore my creativity, as well as influenced me to pursue a career in dietetics so I can use food to heal rather than simply piling on another medication.

Think about an academic subject that inspires you.
Describe how you have furthered this interest inside
and/or outside of the classroom. (350 words)

My sophomore year a nutritionist came to talk to my high school's athletes. She showed us the documentary *Super Size Me*, in which the filmmaker tested the repercussions of a "McDonald's only" diet on himself. What I found most disturbing was that the more "super-sized" meals he ate, the more he craved them, despite his weight and cholesterol levels increasing significantly.

Intrigued, I looked into similar documentaries. *Hungry for Change* made me think about eating foods purposefully rather than mindlessly; *GMO OMG* educated me about the history of genetically modified organisms and their possible repercussions on future generations. Then I watched *Cowspiracy* and learned that in California alone, we each use about 1,500 gallons of water a day, half of which goes to the production of meat and dairy products. I also read *How Not to Die*, which noted numerous case studies showing the effects of nutrition when used to defend against top killers such as heart disease and diabetes. Online lectures encouraged me to implement more colorful vegetables into my diet for their micronutrient content and taught me about the grains that sustained ancient civilizations.

The more I learned about nutrition, the more I saw the correlation between how I felt after chowing down on chocolate chip pancakes with bacon versus a Greek salad with a tahini dressing. Since I had started to fatigue during workouts, I considered if a plant-based diet would have an effect on my athletic performance. It did.

By attending SoCal VegFest I got the opportunity to hear food experts in person. I listened to lectures by plant-based doctors and volunteered my junior year at the authors booth and also photographed the event. Meeting others who understand the positive effects of nutrition, I no longer feel alienated for caring so much about my diet. I loved the experience so much that I volunteered again my senior year and also helped with the preliminary stages of planning the event.

Learning about the power of nutrition has compelled me to spread the knowledge of healing from within to others as a dietitian.

This essay proves that "small" moments can have a profound impact and tell us a lot about you.

Tell us about the most significant challenge you've faced or something important that didn't go according to plan. How did you manage the situation? (200-250 words)

I identified the correct mouse and brought her cage to the lab. A sense of dread set in my stomach as I reached overhead to grab what I call the "gas box." Reluctantly, I took the mouse out of her cage and placed her inside the box. After connecting the carbon dioxide tube, my hands just wouldn't twist the valve. Even though I had no problem watching the professor go through the procedure and dissecting dead animals, actually killing an innocent mouse myself was much more difficult. I don't want to kill anything. I reminded myself that I had to suffocate the mouse in order to perform a necropsy to collect organs and record data for research. Still, I couldn't do it. I told myself that suffocation through carbon dioxide was the quickest and most painless method. I then quietly apologized to the mouse before turning on the gas and made sure that it was low pressure so she would pass out first. A few minutes later, her eyes were still wide open, and the lower left paw twitched a few times, but there was no pulse. I had done it.

Even after the necropsy, I was still unnerved, yet I had managed to overcome my greatest fear of killing a living being. This doesn't mean that now I have no qualms suffocating mice—I still get squeamish just thinking about it—but I better understand that in order to conduct research, big sacrifices are necessary.

A good portion of the first draft of this essay remains in the final—a sign that the writer was tapping into a topic that was meaningful to him.

What's your favorite word and why? (200–300 words)

As an underclassman, I frequently experienced social anxiety. I also browsed the Internet regularly, and in some online circles, the word "robot" was used to refer to someone who lacked social and life skills. My anxiety tried to convince me that I was becoming a robot, but I wouldn't let that happen. I wanted change. I wanted to be confident, sociable and proactive. So, I adopted "sentient" as my username. In doing so, I was rejecting my fear that I was becoming "one of them." I had achieved sentience, if you will.

"Sentient" is also evocative of science fiction imagery, from the buggers of *Ender's Game* to the android Data of *Star Trek*. But in spite of what I associate with the word, its very definition is human. We are sentient—we are human beings who think and feel.

And it is this definition that sticks in my mind. Growing up in a secular household while attending a Lutheran school gave me time to develop my own beliefs. Although many of my friends are religious, I think I can accept an atheistic worldview. I can accept evolution and the Big Bang Theory. I can accept, in response to C.S. Lewis' "Jesus Trilemma," that Jesus was neither God nor aware of it. I can accept that our lives hold no intrinsic meaning, that nothing awaits us when we die, and that we are insignificant against the backdrop of an unimaginably vast universe.

But we are sentient. Our physical bodies may be nothing more than complex systems of chemical reactions, machines of flesh and bone, but consciousness is a phenomenon that evades scientific explanation. It is what makes everything significant. It is the one irrefutable piece of evidence for the existence of the spiritual. And this is why I love the word.

When this student's parents learned that she was using Target as her "world," they were not too thrilled. I asked them to step back and let their daughter write her essay. The result was this incredibly revealing, insightful, and powerful essay:

PROMPT

Describe the world you come from, and tell us how your world has shaped your dreams and aspirations.

[1000 words total between this and another essay]

For some, it's the floral perfume of a beloved grandma or the aroma of freshly brewed coffee that welcomes them to their happy place. For me, it's the oozy smell of cheese pizza riding on the burst of refrigerated air as automatic doors part for my arrival.

Target.

Bright lights flash above advertising what the current season brings, whether it's rainbow-colored highlighters or the newest Disney princess costume for Halloween. My first stop is always the dollar section, where I run my fingers over tacky pink and periwinkle trinkets and king-size Mr. Goodbars. Then I circle the white faux-marble road that leads me around my Land of Oz. In the food section, I pretend I'm the head chef of a Michelin-starred restaurant, getting the basil I need for my signature pesto pasta.

In the clothing section, I'm an explorer in a forest of fabrics, grazing my hands on the diverse foliage of cotton, polyester, and chiffon.

I rarely buy anything when I go to Target, except the basil. I go there because I need something, even though I know I won't find it on the shelves. Target has order. Everything has its place unlike the chaos in my home when I was younger. A raised voice, a shattering dish—any noise made me jump to my feet. I spent many nights sitting on the stairs listening instead of lying in bed sleeping. I wanted to know if there'd be an empty seat at the breakfast table the next morning. During that time, I learned how to ride a bike and began going for rides every weekend. I initially chose Target as my destination because it was a comfortable distance. I began to go weekly because seeing the sparkle of the jewelry section, the big red carts, and all the different people made me happy.

As I grew older, I started to nestle in the mini-Pizza Hut and write in an empty composition book I'd found in my dad's office. Finally, I was able to release the adventures that bounced in my head. Observing quietly, I'd find my characters in the somber face of a man whom I'd transform into a painter, or the woman in a retro paisley shirt whom I'd make a magician. Writing, just like being in Target, gave me not only a place for expression but also a comforting sense of control.

To this day, I return to Target partly because it's become a habit. Sometimes it's to quell my anxiety, like the day before I took the SAT. Sometimes it's to celebrate an accomplishment by picking up my favorite treat: a big box of Target's Coconut Dreams (a.k.a. knock-off of Girl Scout's Samoas). And sometimes it's just to get some basil because I feel like cooking.

Target is where the seeds of my mental stamina took root—where both my imagination and my ability to take care of myself found the space to grow. These experiences are not only personally meaningful to me, but Target is also where my love of writing began. The stories I first wrote in the Pizza Hut led to my stint on my high school paper, and now I'm considering pursuing a career in journalism so I can continue drawing from the real stories unfolding around me to shape my own world.

This student was applying to the music program at Williams College. The campus is not too far from Tanglewood Music Center, where the Boston Symphony Orchestra holds its summer academy for advanced musical study.

PROMPT

Imagine looking through a window at any environment that is particularly significant to you. Reflect on the scene, paying close attention to the relation between what you are seeing and why it is meaningful to you. (300 words)

Wooden beams reach and crisscross, arching like a curled petal above me, where spotlights shine calm blue-purple circles upon white tarps stretched tight across the ceiling. My eyes adjust slowly and focus on a lighted wedge rising from the vast expanse of darkness. In the center, the frail conductor leans on an office chair, impatiently waving his baton. Deep-red and orange strings and shining gold brass push and pull at the frantic notes of the finale to Tchaikovsky's Fifth Symphony.

The waves of energy sent out by the tense phrases of this quaint Russian folk tune gone wild travel through the Shed all the way to my student seat in the last row. As I take them in, I realize the true essence of my experience at Tanglewood. It is not, as I had previously thought, a competitive, high society gathering of quick judgments and sniveling musical purists, but rather a celebration of communication and collaboration—the reason I fell in love with music at a young age.

I reflect on my stay at Tanglewood. It drove me, just as music does, somewhat forcibly to communicate myself in the purest form, and—whether I liked it or not—revealed the many facets of my personality to those who were listening to my performances and recitals. I expounded for hours on end about my Russian pianistic philosophy to receptive peers, who promptly countered with their own international techniques and interpretations. As we grew closer during the festival, the traditionally competitive and cutthroat environment of solo musicians dissipated and gave way to a complete understanding of each other and our music.

I hold my breath as the last note of the symphony strikes. I look around, and see my friends with glistening eyes. I rise to join them in applause.

Here is an example of a graphic organizer for the previous essay:

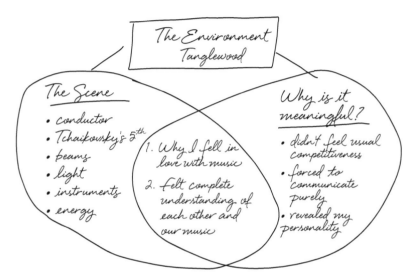

The Environment
Tanglewood

The Scene
- conductor
- Tchaikowsky's 5th
- beams
- light
- instruments
- energy

1. Why I fell in love with music
2. Felt complete understanding of each other and our music

Why is it meaningful?
- didn't feel usual competitiveness
- forced to communicate purely
- revealed my personality

At first glance, this essay may seem to have a topic that isn't "big" enough, but read it:

Describe a place or environment where you are perfectly content. What do you do or experience there, and why is it meaningful to you? (650 words)

Riding up the lift, I can feel myself being pulled to the ground forty feet below. Some of that pull comes from gravity, but most of it is a yearning to feel the snow again after ten months. As I look down at my favorite run, I take note of the ramps and plan my course, estimating the speed I need and noting any obstacles. I look up ahead and see the sign I've been waiting for, "Tips up." I raise my poles, shift my body weight forward, and finally hit the snow. I take a left and dash to the black and white checkered gate labeled "The Edge." It reminds me of a racing flag. *Stay calm and focus*, I tell myself as the slope plunges steeply. I carve to the right and hear the scratching of my skis as I reach down and feel the snow run through my fingers. This is my ritual, turning myself along the arc of an imaginary circle with my hand anchored as the center point. With my head only three feet from the ground and angled toward the sky, I see a wall of snow spray above me and into my long, swooshing hair. I bypass the first and second ramps, which gives me time to build up and adjust my speed. As I approach the third, the wind blows uphill, straight into my face. Snowflakes fly up against my goggles, and I feel a chill on the tips of my ears. I gracefully arc toward the center and let go.

At last, I am flying.

The Edge at Snow Valley is where I thrive: a place of thrill and exhilaration, not just a peaceful setting to passively absorb. I don't come here to simply stop and smell the roses; the rush and tension feel good. When I ski, I seek that ideal balance of creativity and discipline. By fusing adrenaline with my planned-out route, I can achieve that perfect run. Perfection is only temporary, however. At The Edge, I prepare myself to face challenges one by one. Sometimes I fall, and it hurts—like the time my skis crossed over in midair and I landed flat on my back. But there's always another jump, another trick in my mind, and I embrace the pressure I put on myself.

At 7,800 feet, I am able to escape the jumble of superficialities of high-school life and the stress of fulfilling everyone's expectations. I don't have to listen to Susie complain to me that Brian hasn't been talking to her for a week, and I don't have to get caught up in all the over-hype about grades when I wonder if anyone is learning anything. The Edge is where I rise above it all. It's a bit ironic that I exchange one set of pressures for another, but it makes sense to me. On the mountain, it's about self-motivation. When I see Big Bear Lake in the distance to my right and two counties below that look so small, I see way beyond the one ramp or turn. I see the greater picture. I feel that harmony I seek.

ACKNOWLEDGMENTS

Mortarboards off to the students with whom I have worked over the years. You inspired me to write this book and have brought me tremendous joy and satisfaction as your writing coach—except when you waited until application deadlines were looming to send me drafts! I have been especially wowed by the many STEM scholars who began our first sessions by telling me, "I'm not a good writer."

Here's a cheer to the students who allowed me to include their work in this book: Michael Ai, Stephen Ai, Melody Chen, Derynne Fuhrer, Andria Gao, Jamie Hoffman, Vincent Huang, Talia Kazandjian, Jasmin Kung, Biyonka Liang, Ann Liu, Adonis Lu, Vinson Luo, Janelle Maglione, Natalie Marsh, Andrea Plata, Cindy Quach, Alexander Shi, Aaron Tsai, Candace Wang, Wendy Wei, Jacqueline Yau, and Eric Zhang.

Colors proudly waving for my fellow mentors and mentees at WriteGirl, who have helped sharpen my skills as both a writing coach and a writer, with that old long yell to the anonymous WriteGirl whom I quoted in this book, and Allison Deegan, EdD, and Leslie Awender, MFA, of the Education Support Team, who were kind enough to share their scholarship source list.

Let the drums roll out for Vickie Zhang and my colleagues at IvyMax, Irvine, especially Michelle Jing.

A mighty Bruin roar to my English professor, Mike Rose, PhD, who taught me more about good writing than anyone.

Rah! Rah! Rah! to Laura Reidt, MEd, for her input on the manuscript.

A tribute raised in lasting praise to Nancy Cohan Graham and Brian Graham for their counsel on the cover design (almost as fun as evaluating college football unis each season!), Karen French for taking my author photo, and Carol Davis for our "writing dates"—practice what you preach! ;)

Strike up the band for the talented production team at Greenleaf Book Group/River Grove Books: project managers Dan Pederson and Jen Glynn, lead editor AprilJo Murphy, distribution lead Kristine Peyre-Ferry, marketing lead Chelsea Richards, and consultant Justin Branch (third time was the charm!). And hail, hail to lead designer Brian Phillips and copyeditor Leah Fisher Nyfeler for making the book and me look good!

ABOUT THE AUTHOR

JODY COHAN-FRENCH is an award-winning writer, editor, and writing coach. Her previous book, *The World Was Our Stage: Spanning the Globe with ABC Sports*, is a collaboration with 17-time Emmy Award-winning producer/director Doug Wilson. The book won the Sports Category in the National Indie Excellence Book Awards 2014, and was a Finalist in the Sports and History Categories of the *Foreword Reviews'* Book of the Year Awards 2013 and the Sports Category of the 2014 USA Best Book Awards.

Jody is also the author of *What If Your Prince Falls Off His Horse? — The Married Woman's Primer on Financial Planning*, which also won several awards, including top honors in the Business Category at the 2009 San Francisco Book Festival. From 2005 through 2010, Jody coauthored the *Procrastinator's SOS Planner*, which was featured on NBC's *Today* show as a top calendar pick for 2005. As a writing coach, Jody has conducted workshops and critiqued and edited manuscripts, papers, essays, and screenplays. At IvyMax, Inc., Jody assisted students with their college application essays and other writing assignments, as well as trained other editors. She currently works independently and is the senior writing coach at Apex College Consulting in San Diego. Her students have gained entry to their dream universities from California to the Ivy League. Jody is also a volunteer mentor at WriteGirl, a nonprofit organization in Los Angeles that empowers teen girls through writing, where she supports the Education Team.

Jody earned a Bachelor of Arts in Motion Picture-Television at the University of California, Los Angeles. She was subsequently a Screenwriting Fellow at The American Film Institute and attended the Fiction Program at the Squaw Valley Community of Writers.

Made in the USA
Middletown, DE
03 September 2020

17562801R00106